KU-475-492

baxter and sons

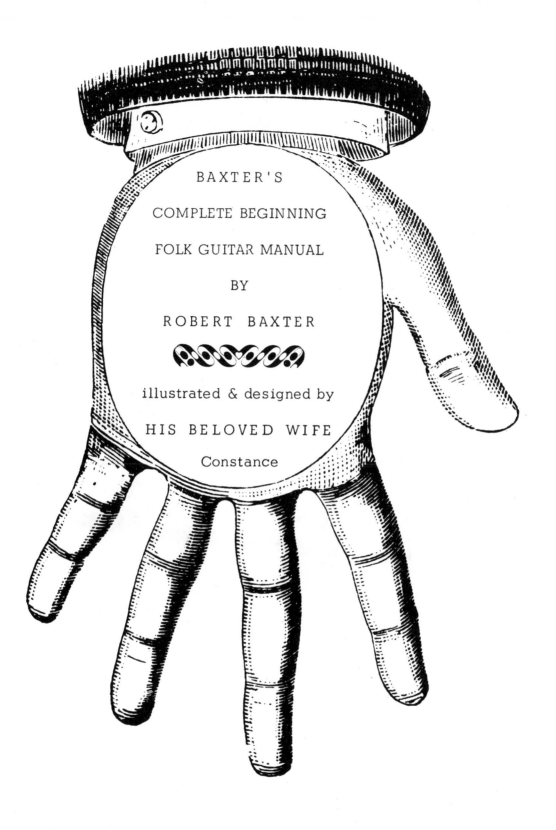

BAXTER'S

COMPLETE BEGINNING

FOLK GUITAR MANUAL

BY

ROBERT BAXTER

illustrated & designed by

HIS BELOVED WIFE

Constance

ISBN 0-8256-2601-3

© 1965, 1966 Amsco Music Publishing Company
33 West 60th Street, New York 10023
All Rights Reserved

Dedicated
to
JESSE TUESDAY,
that he may
learn from this.

Woodcuts courtesy of the <u>Handbook</u> <u>of</u> <u>Early</u> <u>Advertising</u> <u>Art</u>,

Dover Publications, New York.

CONTENTS

INTRODUCTION

FOLK MUSIC today is both the regional "pop music" of specific areas of the country and the personal home-spun tunes sung by generations of families the country over. FOLK MUSIC is the contemporary protest song and the memorable English Ballad; the tune to dance a reel to; the work song. FOLK MUSIC is the reflection of the singing heritage of our nation.

The recent spread and appeal of this music is in part due to the ease with which it is sung and the fact that all you need for accompaniment is a guitar, not a thirty-piece band. From the new "city" audience came new groups with a non-Traditional, a less raw-sounding, less technical, "Popular" style of FOLK MUSIC.

This manual will set down the stylistic traits and techniques that can be applied to all forms of American folk music. Whether you like the Traditional or Popular folk music, the concepts presented in this manual will give you a complete basis for what I consider the broadest view of American Folk Guitar Styles.

Designed as a textbook, this manual should be studied one page at a time, starting at the very first page. Whether you are a "from-scratch" Beginner, or an Intermediate player of several years' standing, the techniques and terminology shown on the first few pages are necessary for an intelligent application of the material shown later on.

Since learning is a personal venture with individual problems, any questions relating to the text may be directed to me, Robert Baxter, Box 605, Topanga, California, 90290. Please enclose a stamped, self-addressed envelope with your inquiry.

Here's a sampling of those performers who primarily use the
styles and techniques set forth in this manual.

Joan Baez	Cisco Houston
The Carter Family	John Hurt
Maybelle Carter	Ian and Sylvia
Judy Collins	Burl Ives
Elizabeth Cotten	Ed McCurdy
Erik Darling	Odetta
Bonnie Dobson	Peter, Paul & Mary
Lester Flatt	Buffy Sainte-Marie
Woody Guthrie	Mike Seeger
Frank Hamilton	Peggy Seeger
Bess Hawes	Pete Seeger
Carolyn Hester	The Weavers
Sam Hinton	

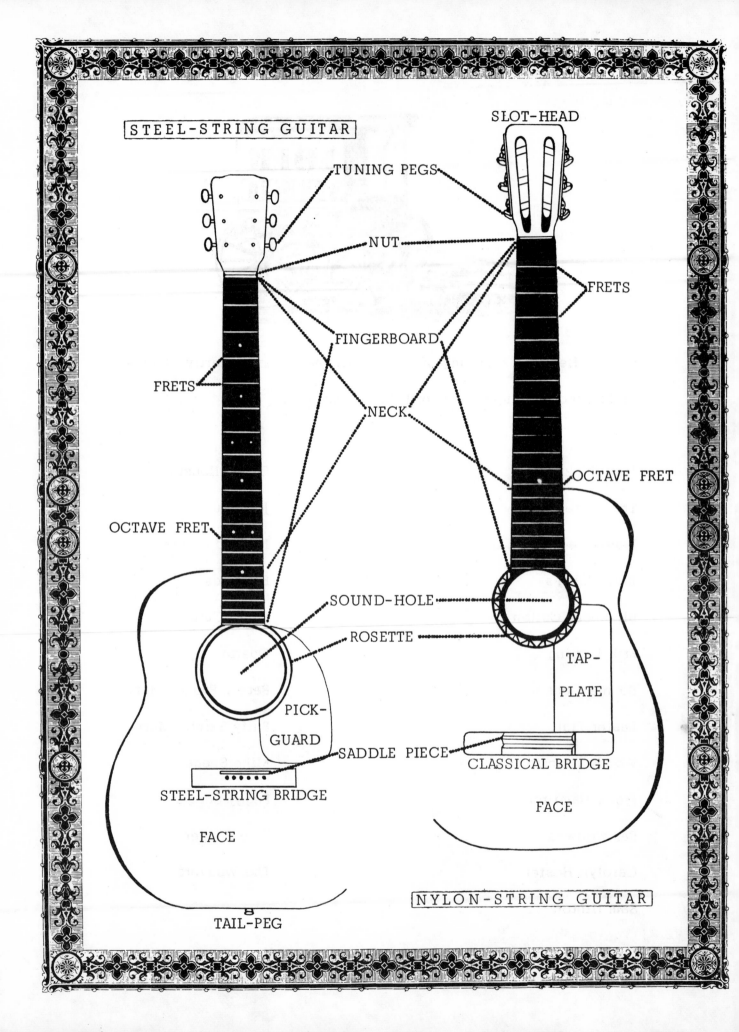

STEEL-STRING GUITAR

SLOT-HEAD

TUNING PEGS

NUT

FRETS

FINGERBOARD

FRETS

NECK

OCTAVE FRET

OCTAVE FRET

SOUND-HOLE

ROSETTE

TAP-PLATE

PICK-GUARD

SADDLE PIECE

CLASSICAL BRIDGE

STEEL-STRING BRIDGE

FACE

FACE

TAIL-PEG

NYLON-STRING GUITAR

THE GUITAR

When you walk into a guitar shop you may see two varieties of guitar. One will have a flat face and a round sound hole; the other will have an arched face, "f" holes (so named because the shape of the holes resembles an "f"), and look more like a violin. The former, Spanish type, guitar is well-suited to folksinging styles while the latter "archtop" is only suitable for amplification or flatpick rhythm chording.

Spanish-type guitars may be built for nylon (or gut) or steel strings. Classical music, Flamenco, all South American and Latin music, and most folksinging strums are generally played on nylon. Blues, Bluegrass, flatpicking melody-rhythm, Carter Family Brush Style, as well as the "independent bass" three-finger styles are traditionally played on steel strings. These – except for Classical and Flamenco – are not inflexible divisions, but useful indications as to what kinds of music sound best on what guitars. While many professionals play all kinds of music on steel strings, the beginner will find nylon strings much kinder to the fingers.

GUITAR CONSTRUCTION

Both varieties of guitar should have fairly thin, close-grained spruce faces. Backs and sides are made of mahogany, walnut or rosewood (in order of increasing desirability). Necks are of maple or mahogany, and the better instruments have rosewood or ebony fingerboards. Plywood is found even in some expensive guitars. It is more durable but does not make for good tone. Most commercial instruments are finished with thin-rubbed, high-gloss lacquer. (Ultra-deep lacquer finishes are very pretty, but measurably "kill" volume.)

The Bridge and Braces

The Classical bridge is glued to the face, the strings are tied to it, and it has a bone or ivory "saddle" for them to pass over. Steel string "Pin-bridges" have holes in which the string ends are inserted. Small pegs are pushed into these holes to hold the string. *

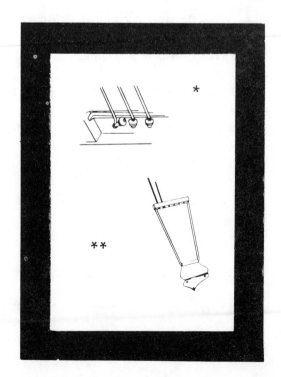

Other steel string guitars may have non-glued or "floating" bridges. The strings are fastened to a tailpiece at the end of the guitar. ** Pin-bridges produce a better tone.

Both steel and Classical guitars have their own particular type of inside bracing. Cram your hand into the soundhole and feel the bracing on the underside of the face. Classical or "fan" bracing has one heavy brace running across the face just below the sound hole, and about eight thin braces fanning down away from it . Good basic steel bracing looks like an "X" with the sound hole in between the two upper arms of the "X" . Cheap bracing may be found on either kind of guitar and usually consists of a series of parallel heavy braces running horizontally across the face. Or there may be no braces at all!

The Neck

Classic guitar necks are just about 2 inches wide at the nut (1-3/4 inches from the lst string to the 6th string) and the twelfth (octave) fret falls where the fingerboard meets the body. The peghead is slotted and the strings are wound on rollers in the slots. Thick metal rollers are the best. The fingerboard is flat.

Steel string guitar necks are 1-3/4 inches wide (1-1/2 inches from the lst string to the 6th string) and rounded on top. These narrow, rounded necks are used for "grab" chords in which the thumb is used (forbidden in Classical guitar technique). The peghead is usually solid, and the fourteenth fret falls at the body. Better steel string necks have adjustable rods in them to control warping (look for a small plastic plate screwed to the peghead just north of the nut). Steel necks also have inlaid markings at the 5th, 7th, 12th and other important fret positions.

In Conclusion

When a guitar maker sets out to build an instrument for nylon or steel, he must decide at the outset which type it will be. The physical characteristics of the two varieties differ so much that it is impossible to make a guitar that will behave satisfactorily with <u>either</u> nylon or steel strings. Of the few models of "double-gaited" guitars on the market today, one is a very respectable steel guitar but sounds like a log with nylon on it. The others I would not guarantee for ten minutes with steel strings.

QUIZ #1

Label the parts of the guitars on the opposite page.

TAIL-PEG (A)   SOUND-HOLE (I)
CLASSICAL BRIDGE (B)   FACE (J)
STEEL-STRING   FINGERBOARD (K)
       BRIDGE (C)   ROSETTE (L)
NUT (D)   OCTAVE FRET (M)
SOLID-HEAD (E)   FRETS (N)
PICK-GUARD (F)   TUNING PEGS (O)
NECK (G)   SLOT-HEAD (P)
SADDLE PIECE (H)   TAP-PLATE (Q)

answers
on
page
#1.

✺ STRINGING THE GUITAR ✺

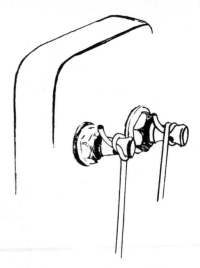

Guitar strings should be changed a minimum of once every three months. They should be changed at the first sign of wear or corrosion. Never wait until a string breaks to change it. If one string breaks or begins to wear, it is a sign that all the strings need changing.

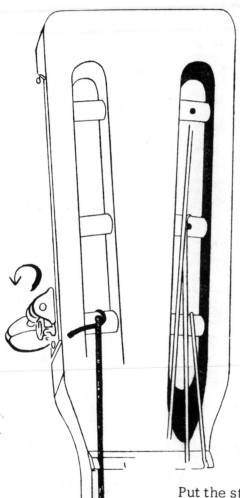

Use steel strings only on guitars made for steel strings. Nylon only for nylon-type guitars. Do not use nylon on steel string guitars to save wear and tear on the fingers. There are several compound brands available that are steel but feel as light as nylon. (If you are not sure which type of guitar you own, see "The Guitar," page 2.)

Change strings one at a time. Remove the 6th string, for example, then put on the new 6th string and crank the string up to tune before starting on the next string. Never leave strings slack to save them. Tuned-down strings wear out faster than those always up to pitch.

Put the string on bridge first, give your knot a tug to see if it holds. Then attach the string to the roller in the head of the guitar. Take up the slack when attaching.

TUNING THE GUITAR

★ Proper Plucking of the Strings ★

Pluck downward (toward the 1st string) with the proper part of the thumb. For tuning pluck the strings as close to the bridge as possible. Pluck with a limited motion of the thumb. Be certain the thumb does not touch against any other strings and that you are not muting the strings in any way.

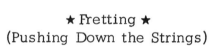

★ Fretting ★
(Pushing Down the Strings)

Strings are fretted (depressed) with the left hand finger <u>tips</u>. Keep the thumb well in back of the neck with the guitar face perfectly vertical. Always depress the strings with the finger <u>tips</u>. (Nails should be filed down so they will not prevent proper fretting with the tips.) Depress the string to the very left of the fret wire without touching the wire itself. Keep the hand curved slightly to prevent touching other strings or muting with the hand.

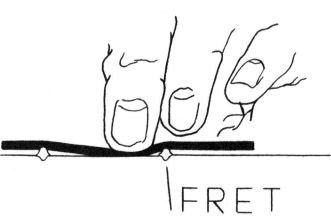

FRET

NOW, plucking the strings in the manner shown, tune each string

to the proper note on a piano or to the proper tone on a pitchpipe.

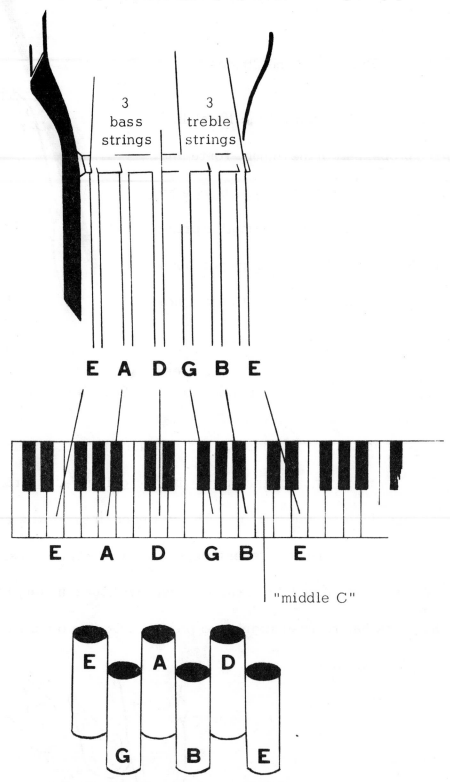

"middle C"

If you have neither piano or pitch pipe, see the following page.

How to Tune
Without a Pitch Pipe or a Piano

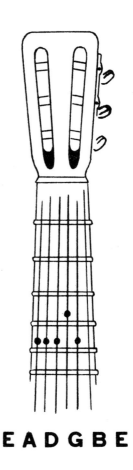

(A) Tune the 6th string (bass E) as low as will produce a good tone.

(B) Then, (with the index or middle finger) fret the 6th string at the 5th fret, and tune the open 5th string to the 6th string's tone. (Note diagram: a dot is just behind the 5th fret on the 6th string.)

(C) Tune the open 4th string to the 5th string, fretted at the 5th fret.

(D) Tune the open 3rd string to the 4th string, fretted at the 5th fret.

(E) Tune the open 2nd string to the 3rd string, fretted at the <u>4th</u> fret.

(F) Tune the open 1st string to either the same tone as the open 6th string (both are E, although two octaves apart), or to the 2nd string fretted at the 5th fret.

E A D G B E

NOTE: If the open string is perfectly matched to the string which is being pressed down, the open string will vibrate in sympathy. Look closely for a slight blur of the open string above the sound hole. Don't pluck too hard when tuning or you will distort the sound and bring about improper tuning.

Helpful Hints
(for tuning the guitar)

It is best to hum the in-tune note and sustain the hum while tuning the matching string. When the out-of-tune string matches the hum, you are tuned properly. Check again, however, in case your hum drifted a bit.

You will find that it is hard to match "almost alike" tones. By tuning the string-to-be-matched down, and then plucking it, you will find it easier to tune, due to the greater contrast.

The most difficult problem of tuning is trying to match the sound of a guitar string to that of a pitch pipe or piano ... both sound different from a guitar string. It is best, then, to tune your guitar to a friend's in-tune guitar until you get the hang of it.

The 6th string will probably not go out of tune if left alone. The thinner the string the more often it goes out of tune. Use the thickest bass string (6th) as a basis in tuning. After once tuning to the pitch pipe or piano, don't worry about being at perfect pitch. Just make sure that the guitar's strings are in tune with each other by using the method shown on page 10.

Tune every time you pick up the guitar; before, during and after practicing.

QUIZ #2

(1) The thinnest string is string number ___ .

(2) The thickest string is string number ___ .

(3) The three thin strings are called the _____ strings.

(4) The three thick or "wrapped" strings are called the

_____ strings.

(5) The tuning for guitar (from the 1st string) is

__ __ __ __ __ __ .   answers on page 27.

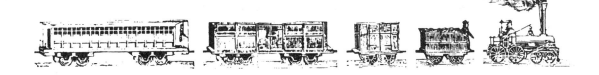

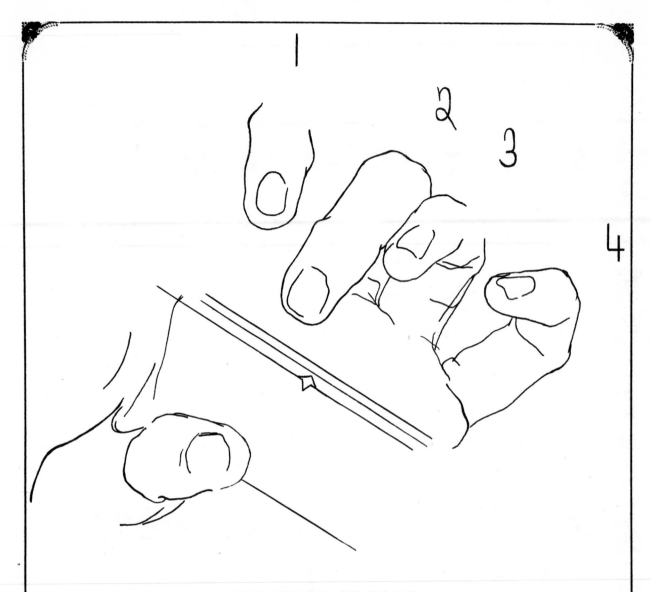

THE FIRST CHORDS

The fingers of the left hand are: 1 = index, 2 = middle, 3 = ring, and, 4 = little finger. The thumb is kept in back of the chord, parallel to the frets, straight up with no bend in the joint. Push against the back of the neck with the fleshy tip of the thumb. With the thumb pushing in one direction and the fingers in the other, twice as much pressure is obtained as in loose-thumb positions. To the beginning student, this is important, so do not hook the thumb over the edge of the guitar neck.

un-fretted but played

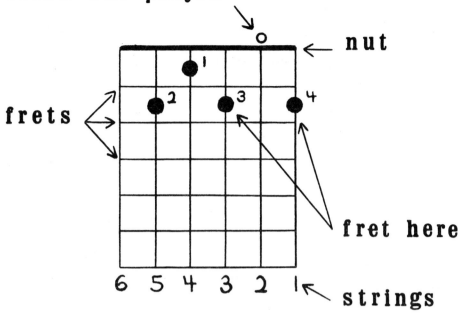

Example "Chord Box"
B7 Chord

New chords are presented to the student in the form of "Chord Boxes," which are, in actuality, a picture of the guitar neck. Each dot on a chord box or "diagram" positions a certain finger of the left hand. Make sure that you use the correct finger (l = index, etc.) and that it is on the correct string and at the proper fret.

The right hand may pluck any string that is fretted, plus those strings which are unfretted but marked with an "o." Any other string (in the above example, the 6th string) can not be played. Such strings are sometimes marked with an "x."

Be certain the left hand is curved so as not to mute the strings. Depress the strings with the finger tips! Now, pluck each string with the thumb to hear if you are fretting properly and clearly. Exert equal pressure with the fingers of the left hand upon all the strings fretted. Keep this pressure constant while the strings are being plucked. If a string buzzes it might be due to your touching the fret wire. A dull "thud" might be due to weak pressure or fretting too far to the left of a fret. Experiment until all the strings sound out clearly.

Now, here is a new chord. After forming it, compare your hand to those in the following drawings.

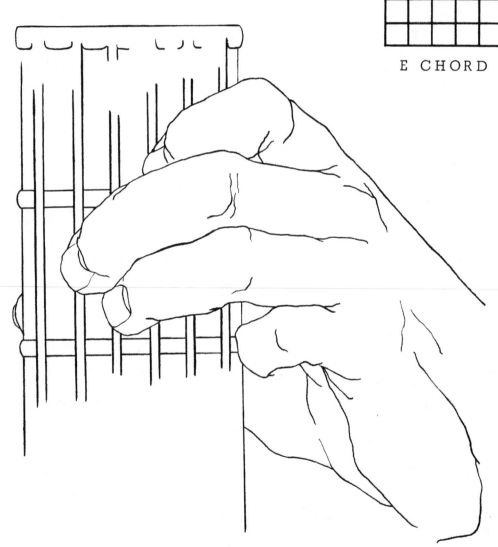

E CHORD

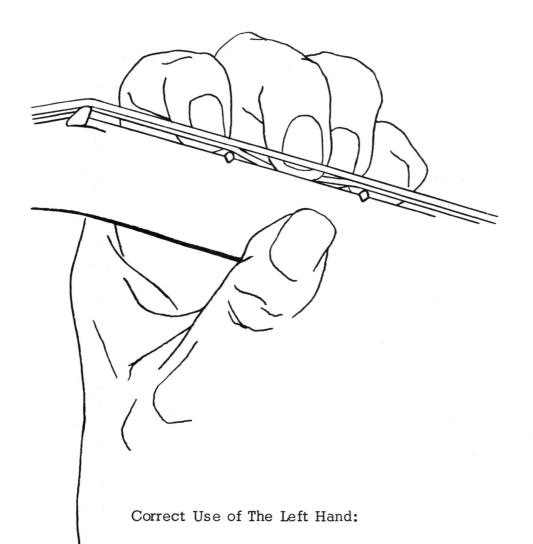

Correct Use of The Left Hand:

(a) The fingers are arched.

(b) The finger _tips_ are used for fretting.

(c) The strings are fretted close to, but not on, the fret wire.

(d) The thumb, although not directly in the center back of the neck, is still in a position where it applies pressure. The beginner should center the thumb (page 13). Once you can fret so that the strings sound out clearly, the above position may be used.

QUIZ #3

The fingers of the chording hand are
numbered: 1 = _____, 2 = _____,
3 = _____, and 4 = _____.

The _____ is not used in fretting.

Two chords you have learned are ___
and ___.

The thumb should be parallel to the
_____.

The thumb joint should not _____.

answers on page 47.

Do not proceed to the next page until both chords
sound out clearly with no buzzing or thud sounds.

THE RIGHT HAND

Many times you hear the comment, "It looks so easy when he plays." The right, or plucking hand of a professional folk guitar player moves so effortlessly over the strings. Each movement is precise. Nothing is haphazard, for the fingers move just enough to perform their duties and no more.

A controlled right hand may be the result of many years playing. Time seems to erase wasted action, yet, with proper instruction, the beginner can learn controlled right hand movement with a few hours practice.

First, make a loose fist with the right hand. Pretend that you are holding a spiked ball. The fingers should hold the ball securely, but loosely enough to avoid being stuck. The wrist should have only a slight bend in it. The fingers should have a graceful curve. If the knuckles are turning white ... loosen up!

Now, with the fingers together and moving as a unit, open and close the fist. Do not straighten the fingers, but keep them slightly cupped as people do when they wave bye-bye to a baby. The top of the hand should remain motionless as you move the fingers.

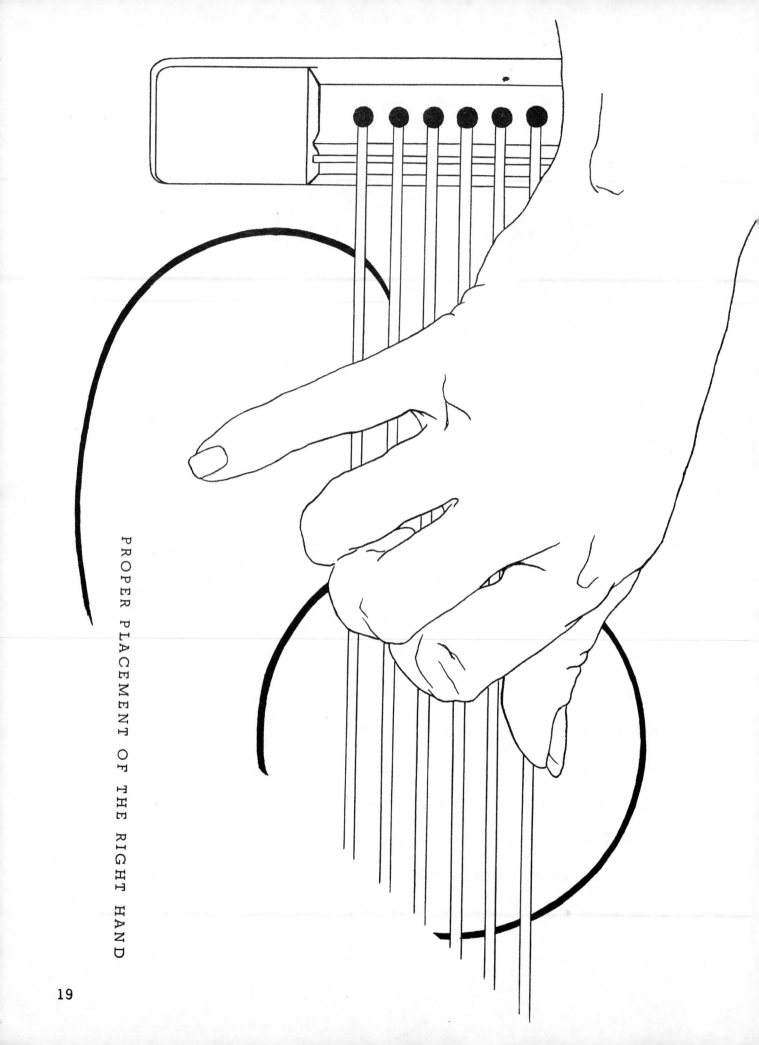

PROPER PLACEMENT OF THE RIGHT HAND

19

Hand Placement

Place the guitar comfortably in your lap (usually with the right leg crossed over the left). The guitar is not to be balanced, but rested on either the right or the left thigh and held against the body with the extreme upper right forearm. Be certain that the guitar face is vertical. Do not lay it out flat on your lap as with a dulcimer. Hold the head of the instrument slightly higher than the body or box.

Rest the right thumb securely on the 6th (thickest and lowest tone) string. The thumb should be parallel to the string.

Make a loose fist as before and hook the very tips of the fingers under the strings: the index tip under the 3rd string, the middle tip under the 2nd string, and the ring finger tip under the 1st or thinnest string. The top of the hand should be parallel with the face of the instrument, with the fingers forming a graceful curve. Now, extend the thumb along the 6th string, away from the fist, toward the head of the instrument. The hand should remain slightly to the right of the sound hole.

Plucking the Strings

Check to see that (1) the hand is placed slightly to the right of the sound hole, (2) the tips of the fingers are hooked under their respective strings, (3) the fingers are curved loosely, (4) the thumb is well extended toward the head of the instrument, and (5) the top of the hand is parallel with the face of the guitar.

Now, place the little finger on the face of the guitar. (Be certain the fingernail is cut down or it will scar the instrument's finish.) This will give the hand a solid foundation and insure correct hand position. With the little finger on the face, the tendons of the hand will stretch and allow the awkward movement of the ring finger to loosen up and be controlled. Later, when you can pluck easily, without moving the hand out of position, the little finger may be lifted. This will usually take a month or so.

With the little finger on the face and the thumb on the bass string, press the three plucking fingers together and pluck up into the hand, sounding the three treble strings.

Pluck using just the tips of the fingers. The pad of the fingers should come across the string first, followed by the fingernails. (Fingernails should protrude slightly. Keep fingernails rounded with a very fine grain of sandpaper because squared off nails will snag on the strings and break.)

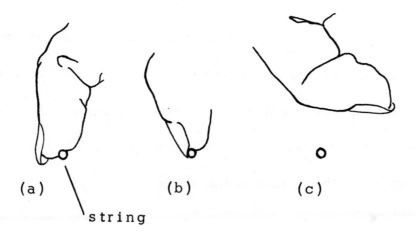

(a)   (b)   (c)

string

If the thumb tends to raise off the bass string, practice until it stays down. If the little finger comes off the face, try again and again until it stays solid or you will never stretch that ring finger tendon. After plucking, do not return the fingers to the strings or you will mute the tone.

The Arpeggio

When the fingers produce a clear, not buzzy, sound and the hand is moving properly and easily, try plucking the strings one at a time.

With the thumb and little finger solidly planted in their places, pluck first with the index finger, then with the middle, and then with the ring finger. (The index always plucks the 3rd string, the middle the 2nd string, and the ring finger the 1st string.) Now, try plucking with the ring finger, then the middle and then the index. (The index finger still plucks the 3rd string, etc.) You will have a difficult time trying to keep the little finger securely planted on the face, but persevere!

Any right hand style that incorporates fingers that sound the treble strings (together or separately) in this way is a Plucking Style. A type of plucking style that sounds one string at a time in a pattern using three or more strings is an Arpeggio (broken chord) style.

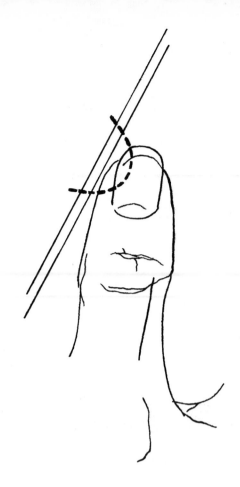

The Thumb

So far, the thumb has rested securely on the 6th string while the fingers plucked. Now, rest the fingers on their treble strings, while the thumb plucks. The little finger, as always, remains on the face of the guitar.

The thumb plucks only the 6th, 5th and 4th strings. Place the thumb on the 6th string, being certain that the thumb is well extended toward the head of the instrument. The thumb should remain unbending and move only where it joins the hand. With the fingers unmoving, and the top of the hand steady, pluck downward with the thumb and rest on the bass string below (5th). The movement should be downward and in.

Now, pluck the 5th string and rest on the 4th. Be certain the rest of the hand is motionless at all times. It may seem that the base of the thumb is pressed so close to the strings that you will dampen the sound, but a little experimentation will correct this.

To pluck the 4th string, move the thumb in the usual manner but do not rest on the 3rd string because it must be free for the index finger to pluck. Simply hover above the 3rd string after plucking the 4th.

Now, try the entire pattern: 6th string-5th string-4th string-6th-5th-4th-6th-5th-4th-6-5-4-6-5-4-etc. Practice until the thumb moves freely but in a controlled manner.

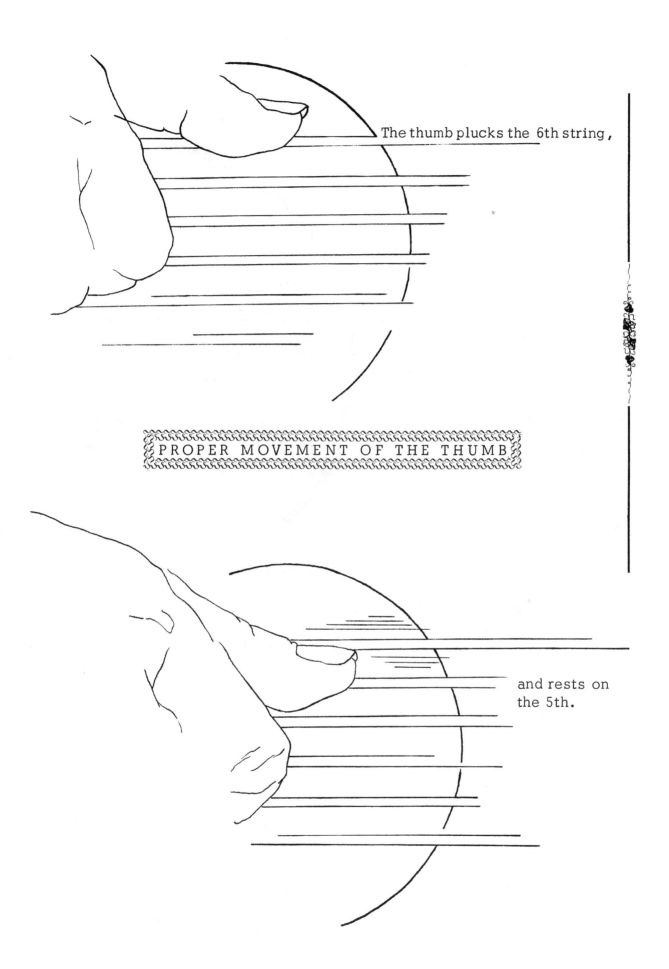

The thumb plucks the 6th string,

PROPER MOVEMENT OF THE THUMB

and rests on the 5th.

Incorporating the Fingers to Form a
Complete Right Hand Pattern

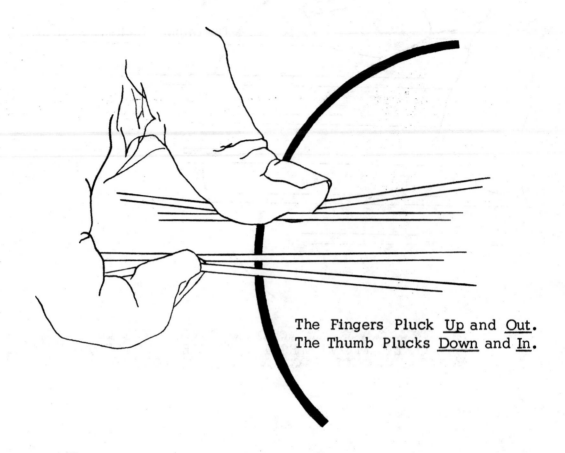

The Fingers Pluck <u>Up</u> and <u>Out</u>.
The Thumb Plucks <u>Down</u> and <u>In</u>.

After separately practicing the movements of both the thumb and the fingers, combine them in order to form a complete right hand pattern. (As always, 6, 5 and 4 stand for those bass strings and these strings are plucked with the thumb. The index, middle and ring fingers (I, M, R) continue to pluck their respective treble strings.)

6, index, middle, ring, 5, index, middle, ring, 4, index, middle, ring, 6, I, M, R, 5, I, M, R, 4, I, M, R, etc. This is an excellent right hand Arpeggio pattern for 4/4 and 2/4 time songs. (Time signatures are explained later.)

Here are some more patterns for practice and use in voice accompaniment.

(1) 6,R,M,I, 5,R,M,I, 4,R,M,I, etc. (4/4 and 2/4 time)

(2) 6,I,MR,I, 5,I,MR,I, 4,I,MR,I, etc. (4/4 and 2/4 time)

(3) 6,I,MR,I,MR,I, 5,I,MR,I,MR,I, 4,I,MR,I,MR,I, etc.

(3/4 and 6/8 time)

(4) 6,IMR,IMR, 5,IMR,IMR, 4,IMR,IMR, etc. (3/4 time)

(5) 6,I,M,R,M,I, 5,I,M,R,M,I, 4,I,M,R,M,I, etc.

(6/8 and 3/4 time)

In pattern #2 the middle and ring fingers pluck their strings at the same time. In pattern #4 the thumb plucks the 6th string and then the index, middle and ring fingers pluck at the same time: again these three fingers pluck together and this completes the third part of the pattern.

Strive to keep a steady rhythm with a minimum of finger-thumb action. Work on the right hand alone. Do not add chords at this time.

QUIZ #4

(1) In plucking styles, the index plays only the _____ string.
(2) The _____ plays only the _____ string.
(3) The _____ plays only the _____ string.
(4) The thumb plays the _____, _____ and _____ strings.
(5) The little finger _____.
(6) After plucking the 6th or the 5th string, the thumb rests on ____
    _____.
(7) After plucking the 4th string, the thumb _____.
(8) The top of the hand _____.
(9) The fingers pluck up and _____. The thumb plucks _____
    and ____.
(10) The right hand fingernails should be _____.

answers on page 36.

answers to quiz #2

(1) one.

(2) six.

(3) treble

(4) bass

(5) E B G D A E

THE FIRST TUNE

In order to further acquaint you with the movement of the fingers, and help you to maintain a thumb that rests properly on a bass string while the fingers pluck ... here is a short tune.

Follow the preparatory directions step-by-step and do not go on to the next section until you can play the piece smoothly and with no mistakes. Do not regard the piece as finished until you can play it effortlessly and perfectly several times in succession. And don't rush!

(1) Place the right hand in the proper position, as outlined previously.

  (a) ring finger on 1st, E string.
  (b) middle finger on 2nd, B string.
  (c) index finger on 3rd, G string.
  (d) little finger on face.
  (e) thumb resting on 5th, A string.

The thumb does not pluck in this piece, but must be rested on the 5th string throughout. The little finger must stay on the face. This will hold your hand in the proper position, and help stretch the tendon of the ring finger (usually the stiffest finger to pluck with). REMEMBER: The fingers should return to the area of the string they pluck, after they pluck, but should not rest on the string lest they mute the sound.

(2) Try this arpeggio: ring, middle, index, ring, middle, index, etc. 1, 2, 3, 1, 2, 3, etc. In order to maintain an even beat, count like this: 1 (ring), 2 (middle), 3 (index), 1 (ring again), 2 (middle), 3 (index), 1 (ring again). Placing a slight accent on the ring finger pluck will help you keep a steady beat. 1,2,3,1,2,3,1,2,3,1,2,3,etc. Tap your foot in rhythm. Go extra slowly, and be sure that each string is sounding out clearly. Keep the thumb and little finger firmly braced.

(3) When the rhythm is even and each note is sounding out clearly with the hand rock-solid, add the following chords as noted.

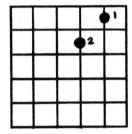

form
CHORD NUMBER ONE:

and play
R, M, I, R, M, I, R, M, I,

without releasing the pressure of the left hand, slide up the neck to
CHORD NUMBER TWO:

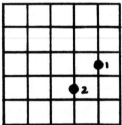

and play
R, M, I, R, M, I, R, M, I,

without releasing the pressure of the left hand, slide back to
CHORD NUMBER ONE:

and play
R, M, I, R, M, I, R, M, I,

slide to
CHORD NUMBER TWO:

and play
R, M, I, R, M, I, R, M, I,

back to
CHORD NUMBER ONE:

and play
R, M, I, R, M, I, R, M, I,

If the left hand fingers do not release their pressure as you change chords, you should hear a _slur_ sound. The following tune requires this sound, and the technique is an aid to beginners. During the entire piece do not remove fingers #1 or #2 from the strings, and you will find that the piece sounds better and that it is easier to play. Practice going from chord box one to chord box two over and over until you hear the slur sound going both from one to two and from two to one. Be certain to maintain the rhythm while changing chords. Don't let the extra sound of the slur count as a beat.

Notes:

In the following piece, chords number seven and eight are fingered by a technique called BARRING, i.e., a single finger frets several strings at the same time. Typically, all six strings are fretted by the same finger, a hard task for the beginner. Here, you need only fret the three strings noted (1st, 2nd, 3rd) because they are the only ones played in the piece. Simply lay the flat of the index finger across the three strings, pushing down as close to the fret wire as you can without actually touching the fret wire. Push down with the left edge of the finger (toward the head), as this portion of the finger is flatter than the underside. At first it will be difficult to produce a clear tone on all three strings and the hand will hurt and get tired. If the pad of the thumb is directly behind the barred strings and parallel to the fret, its pressure will increase clarity. But remember, you have only played a few hours and haven't had time to build strong hands. Practice and later you will be able to barre all six strings, as illustrated below.

(Application and barred-chord theory will be explained later.)

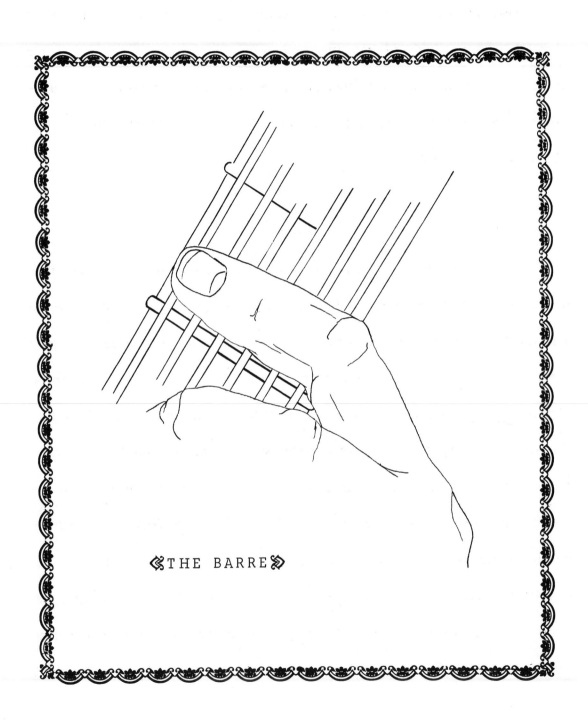

≪THE BARRE≫

FIRST PIECE

form
CHORD ONE

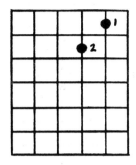

and play
R,M,I,R,M,I,R,M,I,

slide to
CHORD TWO

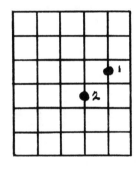

and play
R,M,I,R,M,I,R,M,I,

slide back to
CHORD ONE

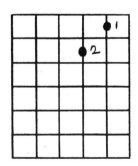

R,M,I,R,M,I,R,M,I,

CHORD THREE
(add a finger)

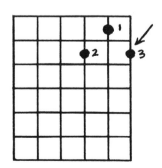

R,M,I,

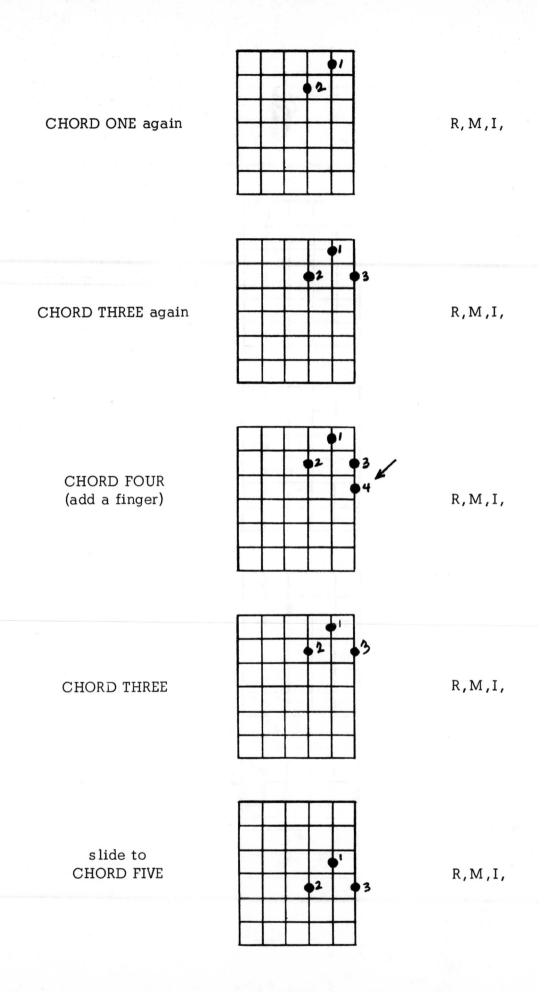

CHORD ONE again   R, M, I,

CHORD THREE again   R, M, I,

CHORD FOUR
(add a finger)   R, M, I,

CHORD THREE   R, M, I,

slide to
CHORD FIVE   R, M, I,

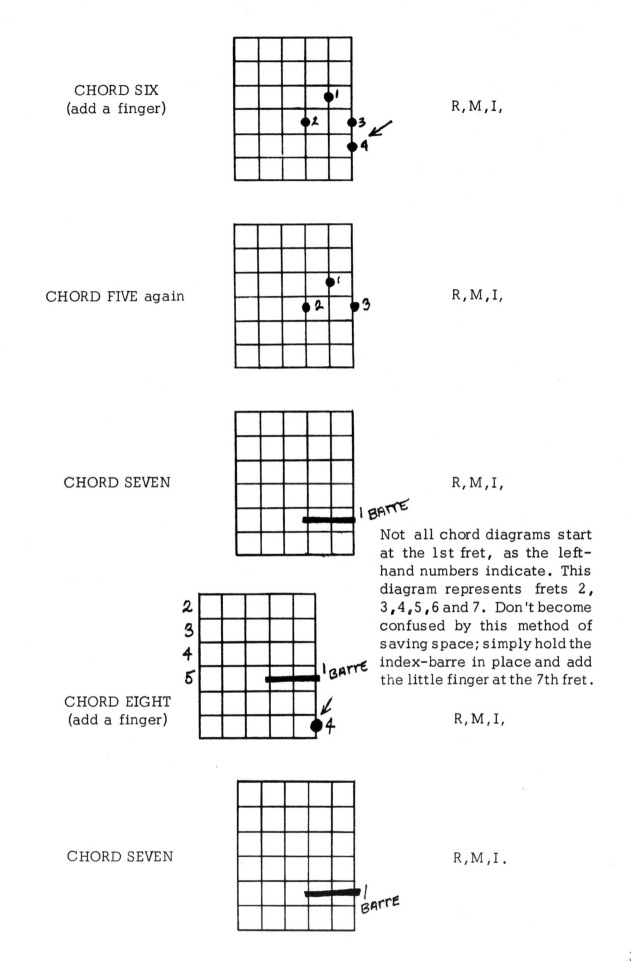

CHORD SIX
(add a finger)

R, M, I,

CHORD FIVE again

R, M, I,

CHORD SEVEN

R, M, I,

1 BARRE

Not all chord diagrams start at the 1st fret, as the left-hand numbers indicate. This diagram represents frets 2, 3, 4, 5, 6 and 7. Don't become confused by this method of saving space; simply hold the index-barre in place and add the little finger at the 7th fret.

CHORD EIGHT
(add a finger)

R, M, I,

CHORD SEVEN

R, M, I.

1 BARRE

34

Keep the rhythm uniform throughout the entire piece. If there are breaks where you change chords, slow down until the piece sounds even and flowing.

In some chords you will notice that there are two fingers on one string. This is because using a free finger for the second tone is faster than moving the finger already in use; and when the piece returns to the first tone, if you have not removed the first finger, you will be ready, simply by lifting the second finger.

After playing this piece several times your fingers may hurt. To toughen the finger tips, try soaking your hand in alum diluted in warm water. Do not stop playing when the hands hurt. If you do stop you will never toughen the finger tips. Play a little bit every day and the tenderness ought to go away in three or four days.

 IMPORTANT

Keep the right hand thumb on the 5th string and the little finger on the guitar face. This piece is designed to aid you in doing this. Do not consider the piece mastered until you can play it smoothly and effortlessly with the right hand rock-solid.

To check the proper positions of both hands, see pages 8, 13, 16, 19, 20 and 21.

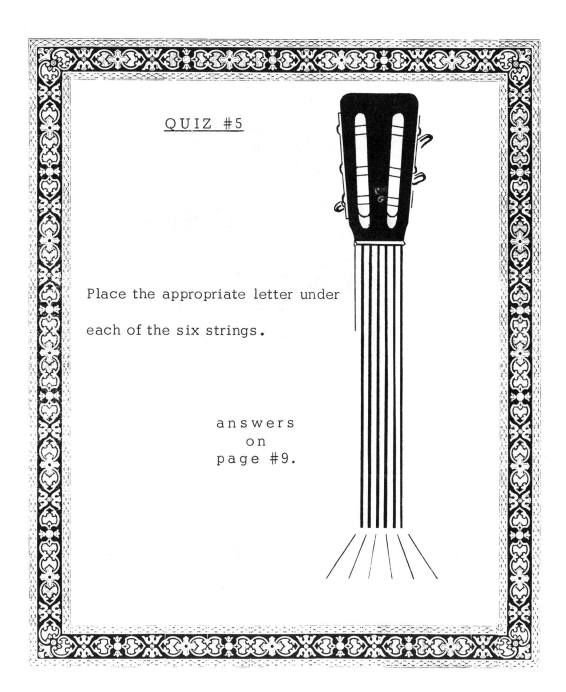

QUIZ #5

Place the appropriate letter under

each of the six strings.

answers
on
page #9.

answers
on
page #9.

answers to
quiz #4.

(1) 3rd
(2) middle, 2nd
(3) ring, 1st
(4) 6th, 5th, 4th

(5) remains on the face of the guitar.
(6) the bass string below.
(7) hovers above the 3rd string.
(8) should be parallel to the face of
     the instrument and should remain
     motionless as you move the fingers.
(9) out. down, in.
(10) rounded and should protrude slightly.

36

Now that you have some idea as to the use of the fingers and thumb in plucking, and the left hand in chording, here are some important facts to digest.

About 70% of American folksongs are written with a certain three chords in mind, i.e., a THREE-CHORD GROUP. Within the Three-Chord Group, one of the three chords will assume the role of the TONIC CHORD; one, the role of the SUB-DOMINANT CHORD; and one, the role of the DOMINANT-7TH CHORD. The TONIC CHORD of the Three-Chord Group tells you what KEY you are in. If the Tonic Chord is E, the main tonality of the piece will be E and the Key is E. The note E is the keynote of the piece. Now, if the Tonic Chord is E (and the Key is E) the Sub-Dominant Chord must be A and the Dominant-7th Chord must be B7th. Every Key has its own Tonic, Sub-Dominant and Dominant-7th chords. In that Key these chords never change, although in another Key they may play different roles.

Now, suppose that all folksongs were written in the KEY OF E. Well then, you could play 70% of them with these three chords:

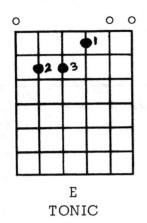

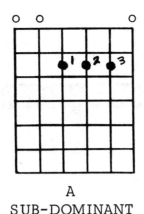

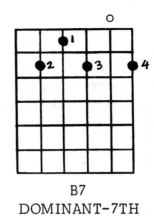

E	A	B7
TONIC	SUB-DOMINANT	DOMINANT-7TH

The Three-Chord Group
in the Key of E[1]

Before advancing, understand the following statements.

(1) A "key" is "a system of related notes or tones based on and named after a certain note (keynote, tonic) and forming a given scale; tonality."[2]

(2) The three basic and most often used chords of each key are called the "Three-Chord Group" of that key.

(3) Tonic, sub-dominant and dominant-7th are the divisions within the Three-Chord Group.

(4) If you know what key a piece is played in, you automatically know what tonic chord to use because the tonic chord and the key are always the same. (Above, E is the key and E is the tonic chord. If the key were G, the tonic chord would be G, and so on.)

(5) Within each key, the tonic, sub-dominant and dominant-7th chords always remain the same.

(6) Although, in the key of E, the chord E is the tonic chord; this chord might be the sub-dominant or dominant-7th chord in another key.

_____ (footnote)

(1) Each key has its own Three-Chord Group. You will learn them all, later on. For now, memorize these chords and their appropriate names in the key of E.

(2) Webster's New World Dictionary, The World Publishing Company, Cleveland and New York, 1953, page 802.

QUIZ #6

(1) If the tonic chord is "A", the key is ____ .

(2) If the tonic chord is "D", the key is ____ .

(3) If the tonic chord is "Bm" (B-minor), the key is ____ .

(4) If the sub-dominant chord is "A", the key is ____ .

(5) If the dominant-7th chord is "B7th", the key is ____ .

answers on page #47.

TONIC NOTES

Each chord, regardless of whether it is a tonic chord, sub-dominant chord, or dominant-7th chord, has a tonic note (not to be confused with the tonic note of a piece, which would be the same as the key). In most chords the tonic note appears twice, once on the bass strings and again on the treble strings.

If the chord is E, the tonic note is also E.

If the chord is A, the tonic note is also A.

If the chord is G, the tonic note is also G, and so on.

THE CHROMATIC SCALE

The musical scale progressing by half tones, or semi-tones, is the chromatic scale. This is simply the alphabet - A,B,C,D,E,F and G - by half steps. (No other letters of the alphabet are used.) A to B is a whole step. When you go from A to B, or upward in tone (ascending the scale), the half step between A and B is "A plus 1/2" and is referred to as "A sharp" (A$\sharp$). (A+1/2 = A$\sharp$) When you go from B to A, or downward in tone (descending the scale), the half step between B and A is "B minus 1/2" and is referred to as "B flat" (B$\flat$). (B-1/2 = B$\flat$) Although the name changes, depending upon the direction in which you are going (A→B or B→A), the in between <u>tone</u> is the same. (A+1/2 = A$\sharp$ = B-1/2 = B$\flat$)

There is such a half step between A and B; C and D; D and E; F and G; G and A. However, <u>there is no half step between B and C or E and F</u>. These are half steps themselves. Outside the frame of this book, you may hear someone refer to E sharp. They are actually speaking about F. And if someone says, "F flat," they mean E, and so on.

Now then, a chromatic scale is made up of thirteen successive half tones, starting from any one of the twelve different notes. (A,A$\sharp$,B, C,C$\sharp$,D,D$\sharp$,E,F,F$\sharp$,G,G$\sharp$) The thirteenth note is the octave note of that particular scale and is a repeat of the first note. The chromatic scale on the next page starts with C and the thirteenth note, or octave note, is C. Start with A and it would be A, and so on. It would be wrong to say that there are eight steps from a note to its octave because two of the steps are only half steps, but the octave note is always the eighth letter.

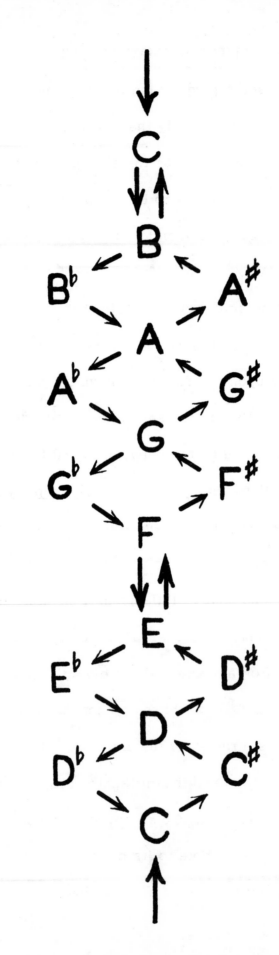

The guitar neck is also divided into half steps.

Look at the 5th string. Open, it is A. The moment you fret this string at the first fret, it becomes A$^\sharp$ (or B$^\flat$). Fret at the second fret and it becomes B.

Without looking at the chart, try to find A on the 6th string: G on the 4th string: B on the 1st string.

On the chart opposite this page, you see that after twelve steps the chromatic scale must return to the beginning note and start over. So at the twelfth fret on the guitar, called the octave fret, the chromatic scale on each string starts anew. (The twelfth fret is actually the thirteenth note, since the string's tone (unfretted) is the first note.)

✳ Twice I have said, "The chromatic scale must start over after twelve half steps." Yes, the thirteenth, or octave, note is the same as the first note of the scale, but it is higher in pitch = an octave higher than the original note.

TONIC NOTES
AND THE CHROMATIC SCALE

In case you need to review, tonic notes were introduced on page 39.

The tonic note of an E chord is E. Therefore, in the E chord given on page 38 there are three tonic notes: 1st string open = E, 4th string second fret = E, 6th string open = E.

In the A chord, found on the same page, there are two tonic notes: 3rd string second fret = A, 5th string open = A.

In the B7 chord of that page there are two tonic notes: 2nd string open = B, 5th string second fret = B. (Remember that B7th is a type of chord, not a note. Likewise, there is a note A, but not a note A7th.)

In the chords that follow notice that the tonic notes on the bass strings have been marked with a "T" (for tonic). Remember which bass string is the tonic note string in each chord.

MORE CHORDS

The following list gives the Three Chord Groups of the most important keys. No need to remember them all at this time. Start with the three-chord group of E. Then learn A, and so on. As you learn each key remember which chord is the tonic chord, sub-dominant and dominant 7th. Also remember the tonic note bass string (as noted with "T") of each chord.

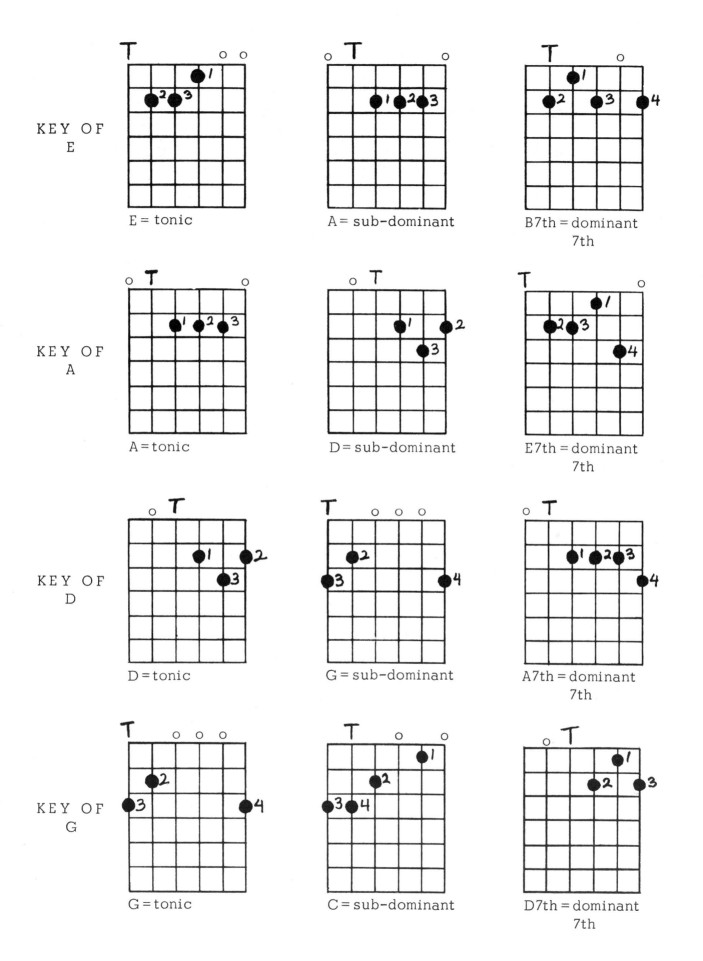

KEY OF
E

E = tonic

A = sub-dominant

B7th = dominant
7th

KEY OF
A

A = tonic

D = sub-dominant

E7th = dominant
7th

KEY OF
D

D = tonic

G = sub-dominant

A7th = dominant
7th

KEY OF
G

G = tonic

C = sub-dominant

D7th = dominant
7th

44

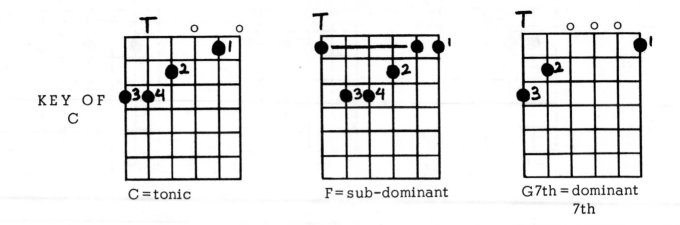

KEY OF C

C = tonic   F = sub-dominant   G 7th = dominant 7th

If you have forgotten what the "o" above a chord box string means, review the material on page 14. Remember, only those strings which are fretted or marked with an "o" can be played ("o" stands for "open string"). Those unfretted or without the "o" cannot be played in that chord. Of course, the tonic bass string ("T") can be played although the "o" was omitted for convenience.

CHORD CHANGING CHARTS

Without using the right hand and starting with chart number one, practice forming the chords you have learned. Change the chords in the order given. Check the position of your left hand with those seen on pages 15 and 16. Do not go on to the next chart until you can easily go through chart number one without looking at the left, chording hand. When chart one is under your belt, go on to chart number two, etc. Later, I will refer you back to these charts for incorporating the right hand.

CHORD CHANGING CHARTS

Do not look at the left hand while going through these charts. Be honest!

CHART #1

E	A	E	A	E	A	E	B7	E	B7	Ė	B7	A	B7	A
B7	A	E	A	B7	A	E	A	E	A	B7	A	B7	E	A
E	A	E	A	B7	E	B7	E	B7	A	B7	E			

CHART #2

E	A	E7	E	E7	E	A	B7	E	B7	D	E	D	E	D
E	D	B7	D	B7	D	A	D	A	D	A	D	A	D	E
D	E7	D	E7	D	A	D	A	D	A	D	E7	D	B7	D
B7	D	B7	D	E	D	A	D	E	D	E7	E	A	E	

CHART #3

D	G	D	G	D	G	D	G	D	A	A7	A	A7	A	E
D	G	D	G	A7	E	D	B7	E	B7	E	A	B7	A	E
D	G	D	E	A7	A	A7	A	E	E7	D	E	D	E7	G
A	D	G	D	G	A	A7	E	B7	E	B7	E	B7	A	D

CHART #4

G	C	G	C	G	C	G	D	E	A	D	C	G	C	D
E	A	D	C	G	C	G	C	D	E	A7	E7	B7	A7	E
E7	B7	D7	E7	D	D7	D	D7	G	D7	C	G	D7	C	G
D7	G	C	D7	C	D7	G	E	D	C	G	C	D	D7	C
G	C	D	E7	B7	A7	D	D7	G	C	D	E	C	G	

CHART #5

C	F	C	F	G	F	G	F	C	F	G	F	D	E	G
F	C	D	F	E	C	G	A	D	E	G	F	C	F	G
F	C	F	G	F	G7	F	G7	F	G	D	D7	D	D7	E
A	D	C	E	G	G7	E	E7	A	G	F	C	F	C	G
D	B7	D	A	A7	B7	C	B7	C	D	D7	E	E7	F	

Do not shy away from barred chords (F chord). Later on, you'll be glad you practiced them.

When you have mastered chart number one, proceed to the next section. Don't forget, however, to come back and practice the remaining exercises. Practice at least one chart every day.

answers to quiz #3

(1=) index, (2=) middle, (3=) ring, (4=) little finger.

thumb

B7 and E.

frets.

bend.

answers to quiz #6

(1) A.

(2) D.

(3) Bm.

(4) E.

(5) E.

first
ACCOMPANIMENT

Now that you have practiced chart number one and can smoothly change from one chord to another, you should be able to combine the Three Chord Group of E and the following right hand styles in accompanying your voice. In accompaniment, the right hand does not pick out the melody (as in the "First Piece"); it sustains a rhythm for the voice to follow. The chords formed by the left hand place the proper notes in back of the voice so you will not be out-of-tune or "sour." Make sure that the chords are formed perfectly and that you change chords promptly over the proper syllable.

Before going on, review the correct position of the right hand, as seen on page 19. Your left hand by this time should naturally assume the proper position.

Now, form the E chord and try the first right hand style: 6,IMR, IMR,6,IMR,IMR,etc. In this chord the thumb plucks only the 6th string because it is the bass tonic note. With A or B7, the 5th string is plucked. The fingers (IMR) pluck the 3rd, 2nd and 1st strings <u>together</u> as a unit (no commas between the letters). If you did not immediately understand the tablature, better review it on pages 20, 23 and 25.

<u>HAPPY BIRTHDAY</u>

(It is always best to use a familiar song when learning a new right hand style. Remember this when you're on your own.)

First, sing the song without using the guitar. Tap your foot in rhythm (I have placed stars on the foot-taps). Neither foot-tap or guitar will fall on the first "happy." Simply sing it and then start your foot-taps.

	*	*	*	*	*
HAPPY	BIRTH-	DAY	TO	YOU	

*	*	*	*	*	*
HAPPY	BIRTH-	DAY	TO	YOU	

*	*	*	*	*	*
HAPPY	BIRTH-	DAY	TO	ANY-	ONE

*	*	*	*	*
HAPPY	BIRTH-	DAY	TO	YOU.

Now, wherever you have tapped your foot simply play one part of the right hand style. (6,IMR,IMR,5,IMR,IMR) Don't worry about chords. Instead, lay the left hand fingers on the strings so they will not ring out. Practice until the rhythm of the song is sustained with the right hand style. Notice that the last two words are played, 5IMR, 6IMR. This means pluck with the thumb and the fingers at the same time. (You can tell that you should pluck them together because there are no commas separating them.) To do this, you must have a solidly placed little finger. Pluck with small motions so the top of the hand stays rock-solid.

	6	IMR	IMR	5	IMR
HAPPY	BIRTH-	DAY	TO	YOU	

IMR	5	IMR	IMR	6	IMR
HAPPY	BIRTH-	DAY	TO	YOU	

IMR	6	IMR	IMR	5	IMR
HAPPY	BIRTH-	DAY	TO	ANY-	ONE

IMR	6	IMR	5IMR	6IMR	
HAPPY	BIRTH-	DAY	TO	YOU.	

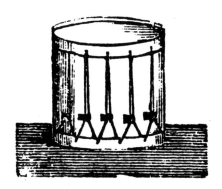

Next, add the chords. At first this will be hard to do, for while you may be used to the chords themselves, after going through chart number one, many times it is a different matter when trying to sustain a right-hand style at the same time. Be sure to go extra-slowly and to tap your foot so you won't lose rhythm. If you miss the chord keep on going. Better that the right hand continues the rhythm and the chord is flubbed than vice versa. Keep at the accompaniment until it goes smoothly and there is no hesitation.

Here and in most books, chords are noted directly above the word or syllable of the word where the chord change should be made. Hold the pressure constant until the next change. Each new chord change begins with a tonic note played by the thumb. This last rule applies to all accompaniments.   Slowly! Slowly! Slowly!

	(E)			(B7)	
	6	IMR	IMR	5	IMR
HAPPY	BIRTH-	DAY	TO	YOU	
				(E)	
IMR	5	IMR	IMR	6	IMR
HAPPY	BIRTH-	DAY	TO	YOU	
				(A)	
IMR	6	IMR	IMR	5	IMR
HAPPY	BIRTH-	DAY	TO	ANY-	ONE
	(E)		(B7)	(E)	
IMR	6	IMR	5IMR	6IMR	
HAPPY	BIRTH-	DAY	TO	YOU.	

When you have <u>Happy Birthday</u> down smoothly, with no muted strings, missed chords, buzzing strings, loss of rhythm, etc., try this next accompaniment.

<u>AUNT RHODY</u>

This song uses a 4-part arpeggio plucking style to accompany the voice: 6,I,M,R, 5,I,M,R, 6,I,M,R, etc. The thumb plucks its bass string and then the index finger plucks, then the middle and then the ring. With the strings muted, try this new right-hand style.

Here are the foot-taps. Do not hurry any of them (for instance, those at the end of the first two lines) because a part of the right-hand style will fall on every tap.

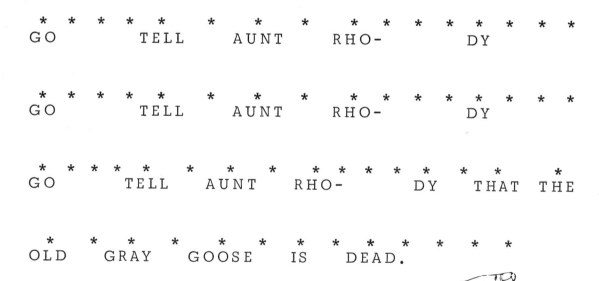

```
 *    *    *    *    *      *      *      *      *    *    *    *    *    *    *
G O           TELL      AUNT      RHO-           DY

 *    *    *    *    *      *      *      *      *    *    *    *    *    *    *
G O           TELL      AUNT      RHO-           DY

 *    *    *    *    *      *      *      *      *    *    *    *    *    *    *
G O           TELL      AUNT      RHO-           DY    THAT    THE

 *      *      *      *      *      *    *    *    *    *    *    *
OLD    GRAY    GOOSE    IS    DEAD.
```

Now, pluck and add the chords as you tap your foot.

```
(E)
6, I, M, R, 6,   I,   M,   R,    6, I, M,  R, 6, I, M, R,
GO        TELL   AUNT    RHO-       DY

(B7)                             (E)
5, I, M, R, 5,   I,   M,   R,    6, I, M,  R, 6, I, M, R,
GO        TELL   AUNT    RHO-       DY

6, I, M, R, 6,   I,   M,    R,  6, I, M, R, 6, I,   M,    R,
GO        TELL   AUNT    RHO-        DY      THAT  THE

(B7)                                    (E)
5,   I,   M,    R,    5,   I,   M,   R,  6, I,  M,  R, 6IMR.
OLD   GRAY   GOOSE    IS    DEAD.
```

Many people who know the melody and <u>can</u> carry a tune find it difficult to get started in the right key, i.e., the same key as the guitar is playing

in. This is such a com-
good to strum slowly
chord before starting
sound of the chords,

mon problem that it is <u>always</u>
over all the strings of each
a piece. Hum along with the
ending with the first chord of

the song. This brief chord-changing and humming will tune your ear to the

chords of the song and get you used to the key you are about to sing in.

MORE RIGHT HAND PLUCKING STYLES

American folksongs for the guitar are nowhere to be found on sheet music. So this book, as you have probably noticed, does not teach you how to read music: guitar tablature is used in its place. But whether a song is written on sheet music for a pianist or in guitar tablature, one thing must remain constant and that is, the <u>meter</u> of the song. So, here is an explanation and adaptation to guitar tablature of the musical "time signatures."

$$\frac{2}{2} \qquad \frac{3}{4} \qquad \frac{4}{4} \qquad \text{Time Signatures} \qquad \frac{6}{8} \qquad \frac{2}{4} \qquad \frac{12}{8}$$

On sheet music, the notes of a song are grouped together in what are called "measures." Measures are those areas separated by vertical lines. The top number of a time signature tells how many beats there will be in each measure of that song. The tablature in this book has no measures, but a more natural division, i.e., the repetition of the right hand style. So, if the top number of the time signature tells the pianist how many beats are in each measure, it tells us how many beats or parts should be in the right hand plucking style. Example: If the top number is 6 (6/8) the right hand style for that song should have 6 parts. 3/4 means you should use a 3 part right hand style, and so on. If there is no time signature, it implies 4/4 time: 4 parts in the right hand style. A large **C** also stands for 4/4 time.

Following, are several right hand styles with their number of parts noted: (Each part gets one equal count. As always, the 6th string is plucked by the thumb and of course the 5th or 4th strings could be substituted. Practice each style separately, repeating it over and over.)

6 , I M R	(2 parts)	6 , I M R , I M R	(3 parts)
6 , I , M , R	(4 parts)	6 , I , M , R , M , I	(6 parts)
6 , I , M R , I	(4 parts)	6 , I , M R , I , M R , I	(6 parts)
6 , I M R , I M R , I M R	(4 parts)	6 , I , M R	(3 parts)
		6 , pause , I M R	(3 parts)

If a song is in 4/4 time you should use a four-part right hand style: 6 , I , M , R or 6 , I , M R , I or 6 , I M R , I M R , I M R. But, which one?

Easy! Read the <u>words</u> of the song. Read the words as if you had never seen them before and you were going to recite them as poetry or a story to an audience. Never mind what a friend says about the words, or what a popular recording group does with them ... <u>you</u> interpret them. What kind of a mood do the words set? The more of a "love song" mood they set, the more single strings in the right hand style (such as 6 , I , M , R). The more bawdy or raucus the mood, use as many strings together as possible (such as 6 , I M R , I M R , I M R).

SINGLE STRINGS FOR LOVE SONGS — MANY STRINGS FOR BARROOM SONGS.

For example, a 4/4 time song starts out with boy falling in love with girl (6 , I , M , R). Girl says she doesn't love boy (6 , I , MR , I). But boy grabs her and tosses her behind him on his horse (6 , IMR , IMR , IMR), etc. You see, the mood of the song changed and therefore, the right hand style changed accordingly. However, if the mood is rather constant, keep the same right hand style throughout the song. Or, combine two similiar styles such as alternating 6 , I , M , R and 6 , I , MR , I. You could replace a part of a right hand style with a pause (6 , IMR , PAUSE , IMR). Experiment! Try placing accents on different parts of the right hand styles. Remember: a pause gets one count, just like a pluck.

More Use of the Chord Changing Charts

Go back to the Chord Changing Charts on page 46. Starting with the first right hand style, work on Chart #1.

(1) Play the right hand style <u>twice</u> before changing chords.

(2) Remember that each chord has its own bass string tonic note, so the thumb will have to play different strings.

(3) Strive for a steady rhythm.

Don't become confused: in sheet music you may see more than two notes per measure although the time signature is 2/4. Notes have different values. Below, the bottom number of the time signature indicates that a "quarter note" (♩) gets one full beat. So, in the second measure (the only complete measure seen) the quarter note is with two other notes, each of which have only half the value of the quarter note. Result: two beats in the measure.

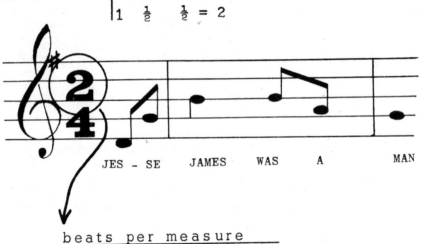

beats per measure

The first two notes are only half a measure, since together they only add up to one beat. (Same as in the second measure.) The first beat of the first measure is at the end of the song. This may seem peculiar but it is quite common.

You will not be concerned with notes or with the bottom number of the time signatures. But I wanted to point out that you cannot merely count the number of notes per measure to find the meter of a song.

PLAYING
SONGS FROM OTHER BOOKS

Unfortunately, most song books do not use tablature. So, you must learn to interpret piano notation in a special way.

First, the book must indicate the chords you will use. These should appear above the words (as noted below). Disregard the notes. You will be referring to the top number of the time signature, the chords and the words of the song.

chord given at its exact place in the song

JES – SE   JAMES   WAS   A   MAN

one measure

2 beats per measure and you need a 2-part right hand style

Measures are separated by vertical lines. The words "James was a" fall within one complete measure. According to the top number of the time signature (2) there are two beats in this and every complete measure of the song, and, you need a 2-part right hand style. You must play a 2-part right hand style once for every complete measure of the song in order to maintain an even rhythm to sing to. The word "man," of course, is a part of the next measure which is not entirely shown here. But, what about "Jesse?" Before the first vertical line there may be any number of notes and words. These may or may not form a complete measure. You will have to carefully sing the song and compare the foot-taps found before the first vertical line to those within the other measures. Here, the word "Jesse" gets only one beat while "James was a" gets two. So, "Jesse" is only half a measure. You may either start playing at the word "James" or you play the last part of the 2-part right hand style at the word "Jesse" and then continue on. (See the following section: "Starting Songs Smoothly.")

Now, accompany this song with one "T, I M R" per measure. You will discover that this right hand style is too slow for the song. It makes the song drag. A funeral durge. Here is how you remedy the situation.

Be sure you <u>know</u> the song. Unless you know the song first, do not attempt to accompany it. You might end up changing both the rhythm and the melody if you do. Here's where a good record collection or folk-singing friend come into play.

When you know the song, pick a measure that you know perfectly as far as phrasing and pauses, etc. Like the measure "James was a" (words are always placed under the measure they belong in). You know, from singing the song, that there is a pause or hesitation after the word "James." You sing, "James (pause) was a."

Now, tap your foot to your singing. Tap your foot as if it were the only accompaniment (do not use your guitar as yet). Tap faster than you usually do to a record or the radio: you're not just sustaining a rhythm but trying now to present a full background with the foot-taps. If you tap fully so that your foot-tap is solid behind the singing, you will notice that in the measure "James was a" you get four foot-taps. Several times try tapping your foot throughout the entire song (to gain momentum) and when you come to "James" start the count for that measure.

JESSE	JAMES	(Pause)	WAS	A	MAN
	tap	tap	tap	tap	

You will also notice that you get one syllable of a word per foot tap and one foot tap where you normally pause when singing the song.

But, the time signature said to use a 2-part right hand style. That is correct, but since the 2-part style sounded too slow and when tapping you get 4 taps per measure, play the right hand style twice per measure.

JESSE	JAMES	(Pause)	WAS	A		MAN
	tap	tap	tap	tap		
	T ,	I M R ,	T ,	I M R ,		

Now that you have found that this 2/4 time song sounds better with 4 beats per measure, you can choose to use any of the 4-part right hand styles.

JESSE	JAMES	(Pause)	WAS	A		MAN
	tap	tap	tap	tap		
	T ,	I M R ,	T ,	I M R ,		
	T ,	I ,	M ,	R ,		
	T ,	I ,	M R ,	I ,		

Using a 4-part style is better than doubling a 2-part right hand style because it is less monotonous.

So, the time signature started you off. It gave you the basis for finding the proper right hand style for the piece. It kept you from using a 3 or 6-part style. And then your own personal interpretation led you to use a 4-part style. Beyond this, your interpretation of the words will help you to choose which 4-part style fits best (remember page 55).

Most often the time signature will be correct. For example, in a 6/8 time song, you will find six foot-taps per measure and a 6-part right hand style will work fine. But, you might want to cut the style in half.

Be prepared to double the top number of the time signature (to keep the song from dragging) or to cut in half the top number (to keep a song from going too fast). If a song is still slow after doubling, double the number again.

STARTING SONGS SMOOTHLY

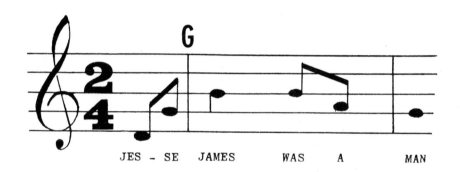

JES - SE   JAMES   WAS   A   MAN

Notice that the first chord given in the above song is "G." But, it is not given at the beginning of the song. Does this mean you do not start the accompaniment until after the word "Jesse?" Not necessarily. For most songs, starting the accompaniment after the singing has started is awkward or abrupt. You can bring about a smooth beginning to a song in the following manner.

Finger the G chord* and start the 4-part right hand style needed for this song (try "T, I, MR, I"). You already know (page 60) that if this song is played using a 4-part right hand style, each syllable of the words and the pauses between words get a foot-tap and a part of the right hand style. Therefore, the two-syllable word "Jes-se" should get two parts of the 4-part right hand style, i.e., the <u>last</u> two parts. Start the right hand style, go through it once and on the second time around, sing "Jes-se" as you play "MR, I."

```
                                        Jes - se |James (pause)   was     a | man
T,   I,   MR,   I,   T,   I,   MR,   I,|  T,      I,      MR,   I,| T,
```

If the words were, "<u>Old</u> Jes-se James was a" the phrasing would go:

```
                              Old   Jes - se |James (pause)    was     a |man
T,   I,   MR,   I,   T,   I,   MR,   I,|  T,        I,      MR,   I,| T,
```

---

* Most often the first chord will be the correct one, but if it is out of tune with the first words of the song try one of the other chords given.

"<u>Good</u> <u>Old</u> Jes-se James was a" would go:

```
                    Good old  Jes - se | James  (pause)  was   a |man
T,   I,  MR,  I,  T,  I,  MR,  I,| T,       I,      MR,  I,| T,
```

CONNECTING VERSES
and ENDING SONGS SMOOTHLY

When singing a song, you do not always want to go from one verse immediately into the next. Sometimes the words call for a break between verses and sometimes you need to catch your breath, so your voice pauses while the right hand style and the rhythm continues. Simply play the complete right hand style two or three times before singing the next verse. Be sure to start singing on the proper beat of the right hand style, as you did to start the song. This vocal rest between verses will help your songs to have an easy going sound instead of a non-professional rush.

To end the song, simply finish the right hand pattern and then with the thumb pluck the bass string tonic note of the final chord. If you wish, you may repeat the right hand pattern once or twice before plucking the final tonic note. Experimentation and listening to records will help you to end your songs smoothly.

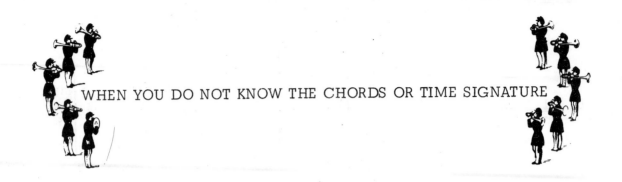

WHEN YOU DO NOT KNOW THE CHORDS OR TIME SIGNATURE

The ability to choose the proper chords for a song without using a book, song sheet, or tablature, is difficult for the beginner. But, it can be quickly learned.

Choose a folksong that you know well and a three-chord group (a key) that you are relatively comfortable with (E, for example). Almost every folksong begins with the tonic chord, so start with that. Drag your thumb down across the strings (all six) in an even rhythm as you sing the words. <u>Do</u> <u>not</u> <u>choose</u> <u>a</u> <u>right</u> <u>hand</u> <u>style</u> <u>at</u> <u>this</u> <u>point</u>. Be sure every string is heard and rings out.

Keep singing the song and strumming until the tonic chord seems unbearably out of tune. Then change to another of the chords within the three-chord group and see if that one fits the sung melody. Since most American folksongs do not use chords outside the three-chord group, just switch to the dominant 7th or sub-dominant chord. In other words, three chords are all you need in order to play a great many songs. The three chords all belong to a particular three-chord group. Any three-chord group can be used for any song.

You have probably noticed that time signatures fall into two categories. Either the top number is a multiple of two (2/4, 4/4, etc.) or a multiple of three (3/4, 6/8, etc.). In order to discover the time signature of a song, without the aid of a book, begin tapping your foot: one-two, one-two, with heavy emphasis on one (í-2, í-2). Now, sing the song and see if you can maintain this foot-tap rhythm. If so, the top number of the time signature is probably 2 or 4. However, if tapping your foot í-2-3, í-2-3, is more comfortable, the top number of the time signature is probably 3 or 6.

TRANSPOSITION

As you become familiar with song books, you will begin to notice a great repetition of some songs. However, these repeated songs are not necessarily repeated in the same key. One book may give the chords of a song as "A, D and E7th," while another may chord the same song, "E, A and B7th" or "C, F and G7th." The same song has been placed in three different keys.

So, if you do not like the chords that are given for a song (perhaps, because you cannot sing in that key, or because a friend cannot play them) you can change keys. But, you must be sure to use the chords of the new key properly and, before you can do this you must study the original chords given for the song. Follow these rules:

(1)   Look at the given chords for the song and try to pick out the tonic

        chord. The tonic chord usually begins and ends a folksong. But, if

        the first and last chord of the song are different, the last chord is

        most likely the tonic chord. Now you have the <u>original</u> tonic chord

        for the song.

(2)   Look for the original dominant-7th chord. If there is one, it will

        have a " 7th. "

(3)   The remaining chord, or the remaining chord that is most used will

        probably be the original sub-dominant chord of the song.

(4)   Now, try to think about the original chords in terms of the parts

        they play, tonic, sub-dominant, and dominant-7th. Decide upon a

        new key and wherever the original tonic chord appears, play the

        tonic chord of the new key. Where the original sub-dominant chord

        appears, play the sub-dominant chord of the new key. And, where

        the original dominant-7th chord appears, play the dominant-7th of

        the new key. You have now "Transposed" the song into the key

        of your choice.

You can see that it would help you greatly to memorize the three-

chord groups of the five keys given on page 44 and 45. And, also memorize

their names in the different keys. Then, when you discover which chord

is the tonic chord of a song you will automatically know what the sub-

dominant and dominant-7th chords are.

TRANSPOSITION
USING
THE CHROMATIC SCALE

A more exact way of finding the sub-dominant and dominant-7th chords of a key, is to count on the chromatic scale. (You already know the tonic chord, as it is the same as the name of the key.)

Simply write out the chromatic scale, beginning with the tonic note of the key (it also is the same as the name of the key). For example, to find the three-chord group in the key of G, write out the chromatic scale, beginning with G.

$$G - G^\sharp - A - A^\sharp - B - C - C^\sharp - D - D^\sharp - E - F - F^\sharp - G$$
$$1 - 2 - 3 - 4 - 5 - 6 - 7 - 8 - 9 - 10 - 11 - 12 - 13$$

Then, pick out the first, sixth and eighth notes of the scale. The first note you already know is the tonic note and chord of the key. In the sixth place you will find the sub-dominant chord of the key. In the eighth place will be the dominant-7th chord. (Add "7th" to the note found there.)

1 = tonic chord (G)
6 = sub-dominant chord (C)
8 = dominant-7th chord (D7th)

At this point it all seems like a lot to remember, but transposing is really quite simple. When you want to transpose a song, you must know the key that the song is originally played in. That is why you immediately look at the first and last chords in order to find the tonic chord. If you are familiar with the song's key, you should know which of the remaining chords in the song is the sub-dominant and which is the dominant-7th. If the key is unfamiliar to you, follow the steps given on page 68 and then check yourself using the chromatic scale method.

The key that you are transposing into I assume you are familiar with or else you would not have chosen to change to it. (However, by using the chromatic scale you might check to make sure that you have the correct chords for this key.)

At this point, you are working with two now-familiar three-chord groups: two tonic chords, two sub-dominant chords and two dominant-7th chords (one originally in the song and one new, in each case). So, you merely substitute the new tonic chord wherever the old was played, the new sub-dominant wherever the original was played, and the new dominant-7th where the original dominant-7th was played.

Until you understand this much, stick to songs that use only the chords found within the three-chord group of a key. Later, in this section, transposition of other chords is introduced.

Prepare yourself for a quiz.

QUIZ #7

By counting on the chromatic scale, find the three-chord groups of the keys of A, C, D and E.

	tonic chord	sub-dominant chord	dominant-7th chord
KEY OF A:			
KEY OF C:			
KEY OF D:			
KEY OF E:			

The chords of a song are A, D and E7th (the three-chord group of the key of A), and you want to try the song in the keys of C, D, and E. You are going to "transpose" the song into first one key and then another and then finally into the key of E.

(1)   When you transpose into the key of C: you will play ____ in place of the original A, ____ in place of the D chord in the original key, and _____ in place of E7th.

(2)   When you transpose into the key of D: you will play ____ in place of the original A, ____ in place of the D chord in the original key, and _____ in place of E7th.

(3)   When you transpose into the key of E: you will play ____ in place of the original A, ____ in place of the D chord in the original key, and _____ in place of E7th.

answers on page #90.

Easy Transposition

Some songs use chords that are not found in the three-chord groups. For example, a song in the key of E might have these chords: E, D7th, A, F, B7th. Look closely. This is still the three-chord group of E (E, A, B7th).

The two extra chords are not new to you. D7th is the dominant-7th chord of the three-chord group of the key of G, and F is the sub-dominant chord of the three-chord group of C. Should you play this song, you would just go ahead and play each chord where it is called for. But, should you want to transpose the song into another key, you would have to know more about these two chords. Remember how you transpose the <u>tonic</u> chord of a key to the <u>tonic</u> chord of the new key: what will you do here since you don't know the parts these chords play in the key of E? Certainly it will pay you to memorize all the different parts of the keys (later when they are introduced), but for the time being and later if you find yourself in trouble, here is an easy way to transpose any chord of any key, whether you know the part the chord plays in the key or not.

First, write out the chromatic scale beginning with the original tonic chord of the song, in this case, E.

chromatic scale of the original key (E)

E - F - F# - G - G# - A - A# - B - C - C# - D - D# - E

Directly under it, write out the chromatic scale beginning with the tonic chord of the key you want to transpose into, the key of A, for example.

chromatic scale of the original key (E)

E - F - F# - G - G# - A - A# - B - C - C# - D - D# - E
A - A# - B - C - C# - D - D# - E - F - F# - G - G# - A

chromatic scale of the new key (A)

Now, simply "transpose" the letters that are over each other. Wherever the original tonic chord (E) was played play the new tonic chord, A. Where the B7th chord was played, you play E7th (remember to transpose the suffixes of chords - 7ths, 6ths, #s, ♭s, minors). Instead of the original A, play D. In place of F play A#. And, in place of D7th, play G7th.

By transposing you can play a song even if you do not know the original chords. There are times, however, when no matter what key you transpose to, you will be stuck with one or two chords you are unfamiliar with. These will usually be the sharped, flatted or minor chords. These are discussed more fully under Minor Chords and Barred Chords.

MORE SONGS

The following songs are presented much as you will find them in other books. Only the first verses have chords and chord changes noted. The chord changes of subsequent verses are the same. The time signatures are noted and you can refer to page 55 to pick out the right hand style of your choice. Some helpful advice, however: Remember that guitar accompaniments sound stronger if all the chord changes occur on a thumb pluck. So what if you find a right hand style that you like, but once in a while a chord change occurs right in the middle of the pattern instead of on the thumb pluck? For example, this chord change to B7th:

```
      A        B7th
      T,  I,   M,   R,
```

In such a case, you should break the four part right hand style into <u>two complete</u> two part right hand styles, each of which begins with a thumb pluck. Example:

```
              A           B7th
 T,  I,  M,  R,  T,  IMR,  T,  IMR,  T,  I,  M,  R,
```

As you see, you do not have to use this two part style throughout the song, just where a chord change forces you to.

It is also important for the thumb to pluck the proper tonic bass note for each chord. These tonic bass notes are marked on the chord diagrams found on pages 44 and 45.

To get you started, I have put a sign of emphasis over the beats that your thumb pluck should fall on. Notice that the first song is in 4/4 time. However, I have placed the emphasis for a two part right hand style, as this sounds better. (You can always double or cut in half the top number of the time signature.) So, in the first song the thumb plucks wherever there is an emphasis sign (/) and on the one beat between the thumb plucks the index, middle and ring finger might pluck together. (T , I M R , T , I M R)

To arrive at your own personal arrangement, you will have to listen to a number of interpretations of each song. Some versions are more widely known and sung than others ... I have tried to give the chords for these. After, you have learned one version, listen to others and experiment! For each song I've tried to pick good representative examples of varying styles on fairly accessible records.

MICHAEL, ROW THE BOAT ASHORE

The Weavers, The Weavers on Tour, (Vanguard Records) VRS-9013.
Pete Seeger, With Voices Together We Sing, (Folkways Records) FA-2452.

(4/4 time)

```
  /         /       /       /       /        /   /   /
E                                            A       E
Michael,  row  the  boat  ashore,    Al - la - lu  - ya   .
  /         /       /       /       /        /   /   /
E                   A                         E   B7th E
Michael,  row  the  boat  ashore,    Al - la - lu  - ya   .
```

(2) Sister helps to trim the sails, Al - la - lu - ya.

Sister helps to trim the sails, Al - la - lu - ya.

(3) River Jordan is deep and wide, Al - la - lu - ya.

Meet my Jesus on the other side, Al - la - lu - ya.

(4) River Jordan is chilly and cold, Al - la - lu - ya.

Chills the body but not the soul, Al - la - lu - ya.

(5) Michael's boat is the Gospel boat, Al - la - lu - ya.

Michael's boat is the Gospel boat, Al - la - lu - ya.

CARELESS LOVE

Brownie McGhee, Blues by Brownie McGhee, (Folkways Records) FA-2030.
Josh White, Josh White's Blues, (Mercury Records) MG-20203.
Pete Seeger, American Favorite Ballads, Vol. 2, (Folkways) FA-2321.
Ray Charles, Modern Sounds in Country and Western, (ABC Paramount Records) ABCS-410.

(4/4 time)

Suggestion for the right hand style:

```
    T,I,M,R, T,I,M,R, T, I, M, R, T,I, M,R,  T,I,M,R,T,I,M,R,ETC.
    Love,        oh  love, oh  careless  love                    .
```

```
      /        /        /         /         /        /      /       /
    E              B7th              E
    Love,        oh love, oh careless love                          .
```

```
      /        /        /         /         /        /      /       /
    E                                        B7th
    Love,        oh love, oh careless love                           .
```

```
      /        /       / /        /        /        /            /
    E              E7th         A         Am
    Love,        oh love, oh careless love                  .
```

```
      /       /         /            /          /          /
    E              B7th                E
    See      what careless love has done              .
```

(2) Once I wore my apron low. (repeat three times)
     You kissed me at my garden door.

(3) Now I wear my apron high.
     You pass my garden door right by.

(4) You pass right by my garden gate.
     But you won't get by my thirty-eight.

A minor (Am)
This new chord
is needed in or-
der to play this
song. *Minor
chords are ex-
plained later.

CINDY

Pete seeger, <u>Goofing-Off</u> <u>Suite</u>, (Folkways Records) FA-2045.
Dick Rittler, <u>American</u> <u>Banjo</u>, (Folkways Records) FA-2314.
The New Lost City Ramblers, <u>New</u> <u>Lost</u> <u>City</u> <u>Ramblers</u>, (Folkways Records) FA-2399.

(2/4 time)

Note: In the first line, the word "pretty," although it has two syllables, is sung entirely on the thumb pluck. "Girl" falls on the beat between the emphasized thumb beats, which you should strive to keep even.

/   /   /   /   /   /   /   /
A   E7th
Cindy is a pretty girl,   she lives right in a tree   .

/   /   /   /   /   /   /
A   D   E7th   A
Every time she sees my face, she throws a rock at me   .

/   /   /   /   /   /   /   /
      D   A
Get along home, Cindy, Cindy, get along home, Cindy, Cindy .

/   /   /   /   /   /   /   /
      D   A   E7th   A
Get along home, Cindy, Cindy,   I'll marry you some day   .

(2) I wish I were an apple a hangin' on a tree,
     Every time that Cindy passed she'd take a bite of me.
     CHORUS

(3) Cindy got religion, she got it once before.
     But when I take my banjo out, she's the first one on the floor.
     CHORUS

(4) Cindy she has bright red hair, as red as red can be.
     She got it from a bottle, but that's alright with me.
     CHORUS

COREY

Pete Seeger, Darling Corey, (Folkways Records) FA-2003.
Burl Ives, The Wayfaring Stranger, (Columbia Records) CL-628.

(4/4 time)

To start this song smoothly: Form the G chord and start the four-part right hand style of your choice. On the final part or beat of the style, sing "Wake." The section on how to start a song smoothly is found on pages 62 - 64. (The section on ending a song would also be a good review.)

```
            /           /           /          /
G
    Wake  up,  wake  up,  darlin'  Corey


      /         /         /         /
                D7th       G
what  makes  you  sleep  so  sound          ?


       /         /         /          /
G                                 F
The  federal  officers  are  comin'


     /         /         /
G          D7th       G
to  tear  your  still  house  down
```

(2) First time I seen Darlin' Corey,   she was standin' by the door,
     shoes and stockings in her hand,   feet all over the floor.

(3) Second time I seen my Corey,   had a glass of beer in her hand,
     drinkin' that ice-cold liquor,   with a low-down, evil man.

(4) Third time I seen my Corey,   she was standin' by the sea,
     four guns strapped around her bosom,   and a banjo on her knee.

(5) Last time I seen my Corey,   she was runnin' down the road,
     hound dogs runnin' after,   bayin' loud and bold.

SWING LOW, SWEET CHARIOT

Harry Belafonte, _My Lord What a Mornin'_, (RCA Victor Records) LPM-1402.
Big Bill Broonzy, _Big Bill Broonzy Story_, (Vanguard Records) V-3000-5.
Pete Seeger, _American Favorite Ballads_, Vol.3., (Folkways) FA-2322.

(4/4 time)

```
/         /        /         /              /
D                                                    A7th
    Swing  low,         sweet  char - i - ot             ,


/             /          /          /
D                         A7th
comin'  for  to  carry  me  home          .


        /        /          /          /
        D                   G          D
Swing  low,         sweet  char - i - ot           ,


/            /           /
D            A7th        D
comin'  for  to  carry  me  home    .
```
_____

```
/           /            /            /
D                                            A7th
Looked  over  Jordan,  and  what  did  I  see      ,


/            /           /          /
D                        A7th
comin'  for  to  carry  me  home          ?


      /        /          /            /
      D                   G            D
A  band  of  angels  comin'  after  me         ,


/          /           /
           A7th        D
comin'  for  to  carry  me  home    .
```

MAJOR AND MINOR
KEYS AND CHORDS

There are a vast number of different types of scales, all with a "sound" of their own. But, for the last few hundred years European and American composers have most often chosen to use the "major" and "minor" scales. The technical difference between these two scales is the placement of half steps within their eight notes. But this you need not concern yourself with. Simply be aware that you cannot use an A chord in place of an A minor (Am) chord. Know that <u>you</u> <u>cannot</u> <u>transpose</u> <u>a</u> <u>minor</u> <u>key</u> <u>into</u> <u>a</u> <u>major</u> <u>key</u>, <u>and</u> <u>vice</u> <u>versa</u>.

Transposing a song that has a minor chord in it is no different than transposing one that has a 7th chord in it. Follow the outlined procedure and then bring down the 7th's, minors, or any other suffixes found in the chords of the original key. Transposing a song that is written in a minor key is also the same. Simply bring down the suffixes. Your only problem should be an unfamiliarity with the minor chords themselves, not with their usage, since you will use them when and where they are called for.

If you see a song that begins and ends with Cm you know now that it is written in the key of Cm. This song might have an occasional major chord in it, just as a song written in a major key might have an occasional minor chord (see Careless Love, page 77).

Here now, are the three-chord groups of two minor keys, Am and Em. Notice that the three-chord group of a minor key is set up in the same manner as that of a major key. Each has a sub-dominant chord and dominant-7th chord in addition to the tonic chord. The tonic and sub-dominant chords of a minor key have an "m" following them. The dominant-7th chord has no "m" and is not a minor chord.

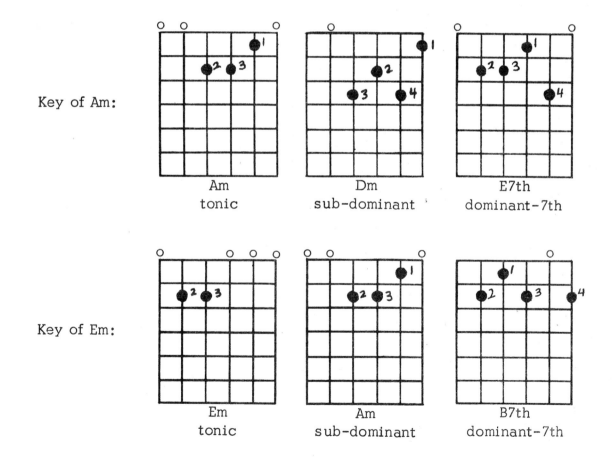

Key of Am:

Am	Dm	E7th
tonic	sub-dominant	dominant-7th

Key of Em:

Em	Am	B7th
tonic	sub-dominant	dominant-7th

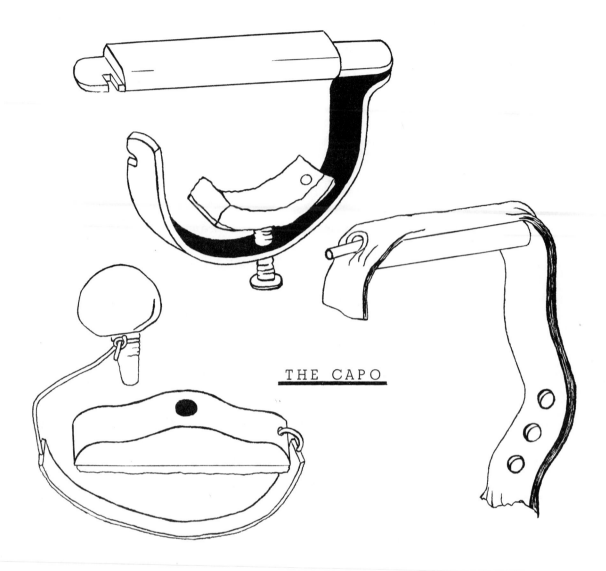

THE CAPO

The capo is an important aid to any folksinger. It will allow you to sing in keys that are normally too difficult to play the guitar in. Here is how the capo works.

Notice in the diagram at the right that the three-chord groups progress by half-steps: just like the chromatic scale. All the chords of the key of A$^\sharp$ are exactly 1/2 step above all the chords of the key of A, and so on. 1/2 step on the chromatic scale or 1/2 step (1 fret) on the

tonic chord and key	sub-dominant chord	dominant-7th chord
A	D	E7th
A#	D#	F7th
B	E	F#7th
C	F	G7th
C#	F#	G#7th
D	G	A7th
D#	G#	A#7th
E	A	B7th
F	A#	C7th
F#	B	C#7th
G	C	D7th
G#	C#	D#7th
A	D	E7th

guitar fingerboard. Therefore, if you place the capo at the first fret on the fingerboard and play the chords of the key of A, those chords will now be the chords of the key of A# because you have raised them 1/2 step. Although you are playing the chord formations of A, D, E7th . . . the end result is actually A#, D#, F7th. If you move the capo up still one more fret the chord formations are still A, D, E7th . . . but the end result is now B, E, F#7th. Move the capo up one more fret (to the third fret) and the end result is C, F, G7th.

When To Use The Capo

When the pitch of a song does not suit your voice, place the capo on the guitar neck and slide it up until the chords suit your voice. You do not have to learn new chords in order to place the song in a key that you can comfortably sing in.

If you play a song with a friend, he can play it using the chords C, F, G7th, for example, and you could play the chords A, D, E7th with the capo at the third fret. (C, F, G7th = A, D, E7th with the capo at the third fret.) The song will take on a fuller sound than if you both played the chords C, F, G7th.

Think of the capo as a device for shortening the guitar neck. It is a movable nut. As it moves toward the guitar body it is said to move "up." Therefore, the chord E with the capo at the third fret is referred to as "E up three," or "G." The key of E with the capo at the third fret is the key of E up three, or the key of G.

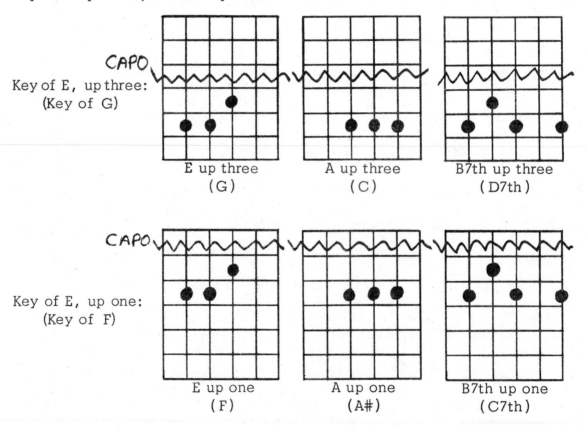

Key of E, up three:
(Key of G)

E up three
(G)

A up three
(C)

B7th up three
(D7th)

Key of E, up one:
(Key of F)

E up one
(F)

A up one
(A#)

B7th up one
(C7th)

BARRED CHORDS

It is generally thought that the better the guitarist, the higher up the neck of the guitar he plays. People watch performers use seemingly complex, "barred" chords and think they are impossible to do. But, as with anything else there are rules that apply to these "fancy" chords and once these rules are learned the impossible is no more. And . . . surprise, you already know the rules for the usage of the "Barred Chords."

"Barred," this word describes a chord in which one finger is used to fret all the guitar strings, in the same manner as the capo stops them, while the remaining fingers form the chord (see picture on page 31). The barring finger, usually the index, is a sort of portable capo. If you had no capo, but wanted to move the chords in the key of E up three frets to form the key of G (as in the last section) you could use your index finger to replace the capo. The index finger would remain across all the strings at the third fret while the remaining fingers formed the chords as they were needed.

This is an extreme example of the use of barring, for most often you have a capo handy. In addition, a series of barred chords is hard to form: the index finger gets mighty tired. So, generally you use one or two barred chords in a song. You may choose to use them for any number of reasons. Say a song is becoming wearisome. The twenty verses all sound the same. Let's say the song is written in the key of C. For fifteen verses you've been playing the same C, F and G7th chords. From your work with the capo, you should know that the chord of A up three is C. But of course you can't put a capo on the guitar in the middle of a song just to add variety. So, when you wish to use this barred C, you quickly barre with the index finger at the third fret, arrange the rest of the fingers and the song once again becomes interesting. (Of course, the actual process of forming a barred chord should not be broken down into two parts. All the fingers should act together.)

So, you see that in a sense the guitar nut, the capo and the barre are all the same. Each stops the six strings behind the chords. When you move a chord up the neck it should be the same distance from the capo or barring index finger as it was from the nut.

By the way, the F chord that you've been playing all along is an E chord barred up one fret. Make sure you understand that the three fretting fingers in the F chord are in the same relationship to the index finger barre as the three fretting fingers of the E chord are to the nut of the guitar.

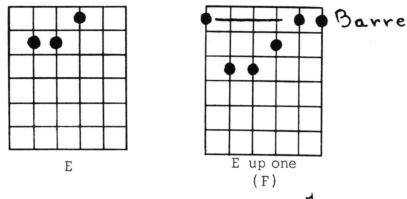

E

E up one
(F)

(If you thought "E up one" should be E$\sharp$,
you'd better review page 40.)

If you move the F chord one fret up the neck it becomes F$\sharp$, two

frets up the neck and it becomes G.

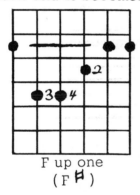

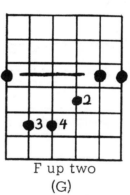

F up one
(F$\sharp$)

F up two
(G)

Barre an A chord up one fret and you get A$\sharp$: three frets and you get C.

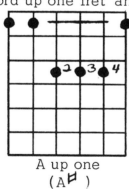

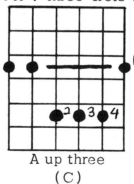

A up one
(A$\sharp$)

A up three
(C)

By now you should realize another use for barred chords. If a book

calls for a chord you don't know and you have no way of finding out how to form the chord, you can barre-up a chord that you do know. For instance, if you were in need of a B you could barre A up two frets.

Most folk guitarists prefer to barre only six different chords. These six chords barred up the neck can be used to obtain <u>any</u> major, minor or 7th chord needed in any key (other chords, such as 6th's and 9th's, are reduced to the basic major, minor and 7th chords through use of the chart on page 154). The six chords are E, E7th, Em, A, A7th and Am. Practice these chords, remembering that in some cases you will have to rearrange the left hand fingering, as the index finger will be employed for the barre. At first you may find your fingers overlapping. The first string will be especially difficult to get a clear tone out of. Try pressing down at the outer edge of the finger-board (near the finger joint) in order to get the E string down securely. (More complete instructions on how to gain a clear tone when barring were given on page 30.) Don't try to memorize every chord that you discover. Pick out the ones that you can use most often.

(1) A barred up three is a C chord.
(2) A barred up five is a D chord.
(3) A barred up seven is another E chord.
(4) A barred up ten is a G chord.
(5) A7th barred up two is a B7th chord.
(6) E barred up three is another way of playing a G chord.
(7) E barred up five is another way of playing an A chord.
(8) E7th barred up seven is an excellent B7th chord.

You can see that if you want a barred 7th chord, you can barre-up either A7th or E7th. For example, A7th up two = B7th and E7th up seven = B7th. Which should you choose to barre-up, A7th or E7th? A7th up two would probably be easier to reach due to its nearness to the first fret. Also, the higher up the neck you barre, the smaller the fret spaces become and fingering a chord is difficult and cramped. In most cases, simply choose the barred chord that is easiest to reach.

answers to quiz #7.

	tonic chord	sub-dominant chord	dominant-7th chord
Key of A:	A	D	E7th
Key of C:	C	F	G7th
Key of D:	D	G	A7th
Key of E:	E	A	B7th

---

(1) <u>C, F, G7th.</u>

(2) <u>D, G, A7th.</u>

(3) <u>E, A, B7th.</u>

HAMMERING-ON

A technique that can add interest to practically any right hand style, is the "hammer-on." To hammer-on is to fret a string after it has already been plucked and is still ringing out. Fretting (or re-fretting at a higher fret) causes a second tone. The first tone is that caused by the plucking of the right hand and the second is caused by the fretting of the string by the left hand. This technique is to be used at the discretion of the guitarist. It will add color and variation to all the right hand styles you have learned. It will break the monotony of a right hand style but if you're not careful it will become monotonous itself. Use the hammer-on sparingly.

Form the chord B7th. Now, pluck the open 6th string with the thumb. As soon as the note rings out, take your middle finger off the 5th string and forcefully fret the 6th string at the 2nd fret. The fretting must be done quickly and firmly. (See the three pictures at the right. In "A" the left hand is forming the B7th chord. "B," the middle finger is raised and poised to fret the 6th string which has just been plucked. "C," the 6th string is fretted at the 2nd fret, causing the hammered-on tone.)

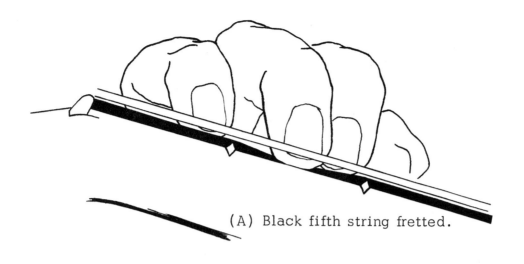

(A) Black fifth string fretted.

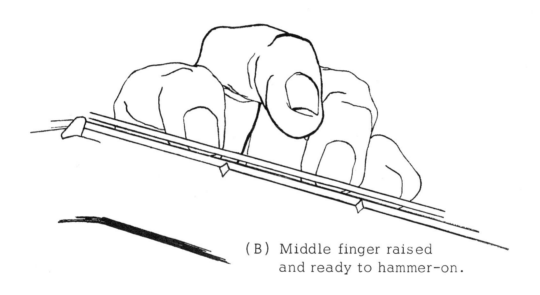

(B) Middle finger raised
and ready to hammer-on.

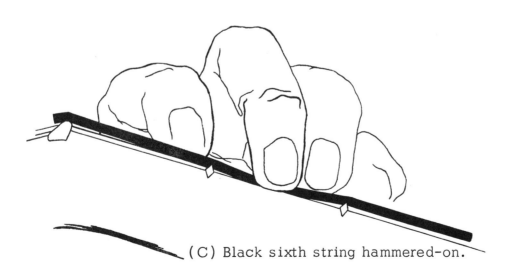

(C) Black sixth string hammered-on.

A hammered-on note should not break the steady rhythm of the right hand style. If the right hand style is 6 , I , M , R and you hammer-on after the thumb pluck - 6 (hammer-on) , I , M , R - the rhythm should remain the same - $\dfrac{6\;,\;I\;,\;M\;,\;R}{1\;,\;2\;,\;3\;,\;4}$ = $\dfrac{6\;(\text{hammer-on})\;,\;I,M,R}{1\quad\quad\quad\;,2,3,4}$. The first thumb pluck without the hammer-on and the second thumb pluck with the hammered-on note take the same amount of time. This is why the technique adds interest to the right hand style. If you allowed for the extra note by giving it a beat of its own, the song would merely lose its rhythm.

Practice until you can hammer-on without interrupting the steady right hand style. Form the B7th chord and play 5 , I , M , R , 5 , I , M , R several times. Tap your foot heavily to insure that you do not break from the 1 , 2 , 3 , 4 beat. Now, without pausing, pluck 6 (H2) , I , M , R.

"H2" in parenthesis means to pluck the string preceding the parenthesis and then hammer-on at the 2nd fret of that string. "H3" would mean to hammer-on at the 3rd fret, etc. You will find more and more use of the parenthesis in my tablature as you progress in the various instruction books. A parenthesis always contains some unique instructions which apply only to the string that the parenthesis follows. Here, the instruction is the hammer-on at a certain fret. If the parenthesis had followed, say, "IMR" like this , "IMR(H2)," the instruction in the parenthesis would still apply only to the one string or finger ("R") directly preceding it. In this case you would pluck with the three fingers and hammer-on at the 2nd fret on the first string (plucked by the ring finger).

Continue practicing until you can hammer-on without losing the rhythm and until you are used to this new addition to the tablature. Try:

B7th
    5 , I , M , R , 6(H2) , I , M , R , 5 , I , M , R , 6(H2) , I , M , R , 5 , I , etc.

The type of hammer-on that you have been practicing is actually more difficult than most. In it, the middle finger of the left hand was lifted from its position in the B7th chord to hammer-on a note not usually found fretted in this chord. Here lies the difficulty: you must be sure that this new note (6th string, 2nd fret) sounds good with the B7th chord. You cannot merely hammer-on any note with any chord. And, while the middle finger is moved from its proper place within the chord you cannot pluck that string. So you can see that this type of hammer-on requires thought and a fast and sure left hand: and this is why the average guitarist never advances beyond hammering-on within the chord.

To hammer-on within the chord you simply lift a fretting finger from the string, pluck the string and then return the finger to its original position. No need to worry about the hammered-on note fitting in. As in the more complex hammer-on, the first tone of the unfretted string may and probably will be out of tune to the chord, but it is immediately overpowered by the sustained hammered-on tone. So, in the B7th chord, you might lift the middle finger from the 5th string, pluck the string and immediately re-fret the string at the same fret. Such hammering-on within a chord is indicated solely by an "H" (in parenthesis) because the fret number is implied by the chord itself.

Try this exercise which involves both hammering-on techniques.

B7th

5, I, M, R, 6(H2), I, M, R, 5, I, M, R, 5(H), I, M, R, 5, I, M,

R, 6(H2), I, M, R, 6(H2), I, M, R, 5, I, M, R.

Always return the middle finger to its normal 5th string position, after hammering-on at the 6th string 2nd fret. Be careful to avoid any inadvertent 5th string hammer-on.

Just like the hammer-on, the pull-off may be used on any string

with any chord: and, its timing and application are the same as with the

hammer-on.

With the index finger of the left hand fretting the first string at

the first fret, pluck the string with the right hand. Immediately drag the

fretting finger down at a right angle to the string (as if you're actually

plucking the string with the left hand). As your finger pulls the string

toward the edge of the guitar fingerboard the tension of the string will

make the string snap back into place. This "snap" results in the 2nd

tone. Do not release or increase the pressure of the fretting finger until

after the 2nd tone rings out.

Remember: the finger is on the string when you begin. Simply

pluck the string with the right hand, then pluck it again with the left

hand finger tip.

The "PULL-OFF"

(A) String has been plucked with right hand
and the fretting finger is being dragged down
at a right angle to the string.

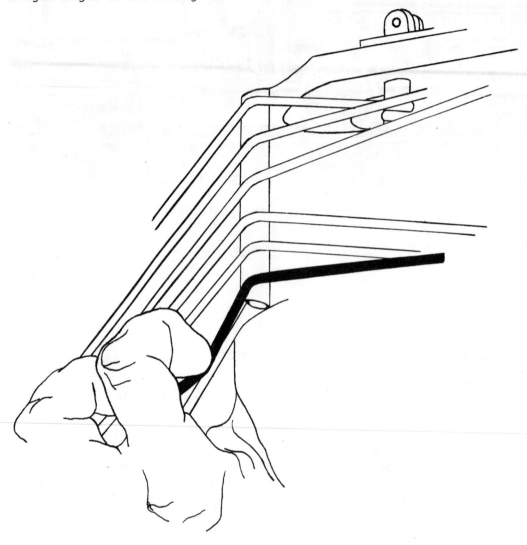

(B) Tension of the string makes it snap back
into place, resulting in a 2nd tone.

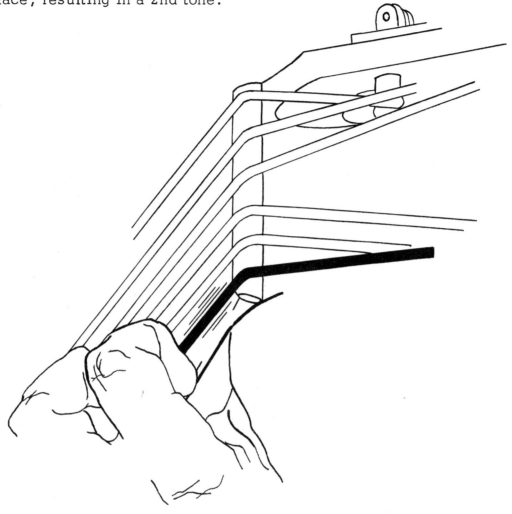

Exercises: A pull-off is marked with a "(P)."

(C Chord):

        5 , I , M , R , M(P) , I , 4 , I , M , R , M(P) , I ,   etc.

(Am Chord):

        5 , I , M , R , M(P) , I , 4 , I , M , R , M(P) , I ,   etc.

STRETCHING OR CHOKING A STRING

Stretching, or as some say, "choking," a string can be used on any string, any fret. It is a Blues technique. Just as with the hammer-on and pull-off, it should be used sparingly. Even a good thing becomes boring if used to excess. Actually, stretching a string should not be used until you understand Blues technique (see Baxter's Blues Guitar Manual). Stretching a string with an English-ballad-type plucking style is a bit ridiculous. However, for the sake of knowledge, here is how it is done.

Fret the third string at the third fret. Pluck the string with the right hand. Immediately push the third string up toward the bass strings with the fretting finger. Keep the pressure down on the string as you push. You ought to hear a "whining" sound (a rise in pitch) as you stretch the string. Push up, then ease the string back to its original position.

TROUBLE-SHOOTING

If the hammer-on, pull-off or choke do not sound out clearly, it may be due to (1) waiting too long after the right hand pluck before making the second tone, (2) not letting the initial tone ring out clearly before making the second tone, or (3) not using enough force in making the second tone.

RIGHT HAND BRUSH STYLES

Until now you have only learned those right hand styles which use the fingers for plucking. Now, some more-traditional American guitar styles, namely, the Brush Styles. Brush Styles are right-hand patterns which use the thumb for plucking and the fingers (as a unit) for "brushing" across the treble strings. Used for rhythm, as well as melody, they incorporate a different set of rules from Plucking Styles.

First, with the hand's relationship to the guitar similar to Plucking Style position (page 19), rest the thumb on the bass E string. Curve the fingers into a loose, well-rounded fist. (In this style, the little finger does not rest on the guitar face.) The fingers should curve up into the hand and not touch the strings. Now, press the fingers together to form a unit, and brush down across the 4th, 3rd, 2nd and 1st strings with the back of the nails. The brush should sound as one tone. Separate string tones should not sound out.

When the fingers have brushed past the first string stop. If you overextend the fingers you will cause the hand to move. The movement in the brush is soley with the fingers. The top of the hand should be un-moving. While you practice the brush, keep the thumb on the bass string for reference and to help keep the hand still. Now experiment. Brush down first with the index and the middle fingers. Then use the middle and the ring fingers and then try it with the index, middle and ring. Each creates a different sound. When your hand is steady, the brush controlled and free of unnecessary movement, and when the tone is clear; you are ready to add the thumb pluck.

Instead of resting the thumb on the string below, as in Plucking Styles, the thumb plucks downward and hovers over the next string (like it does when plucking the 4th string in a Plucking Style), In a Brush Style, the thumb may pluck any string-1,2,3,4,5,6. The thumb must be well extended toward the peg head on the guitar in such a position that all the strings can be plucked without running the thumb into the fingers or moving the hand to avoid this. (See the following pictures.)

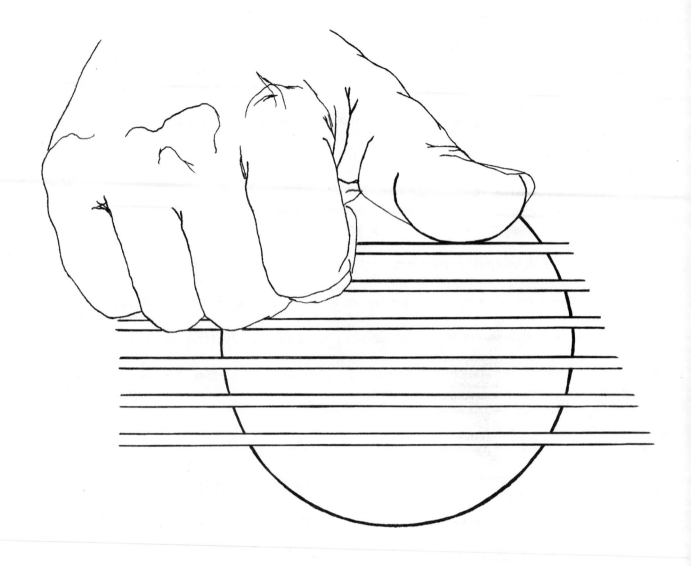

(A) <u>The thumb plucks while the fingers remain in a ready position for the brush down.</u>

Check the placement of your hand in relation to the guitar.

Check the angle of your hand in relation to the strings. Check the

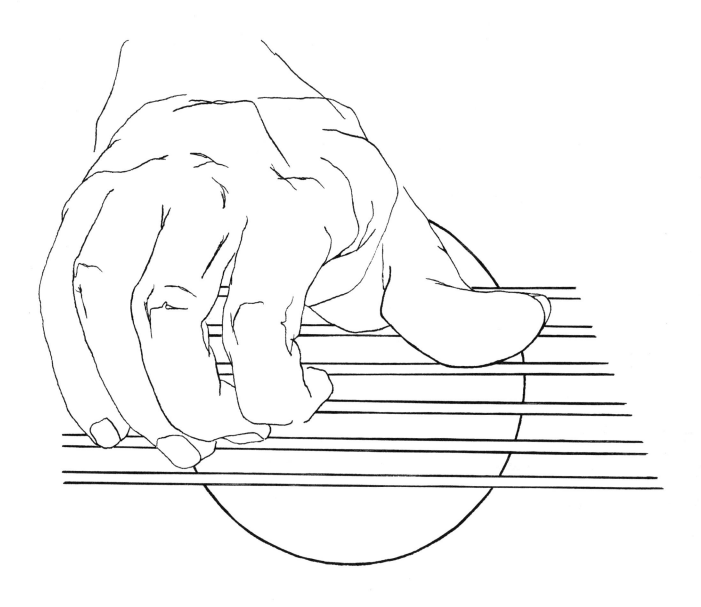

(B) <u>The fingers brush down while the thumb hovers over the next string</u>.

---

loose fist made by your fingers. And, lastly, check to see that your

thumb is well extended.

The tablature for a Brush Style is similar to that of Plucking Styles in that a number stands for a string to be plucked by the thumb. But, instead of "I, M, R," there is "D" for brush-down, and "U" for brush-up.

To test your control of hand position and extended thumb approach, try the following exercise, designed to acquaint you with the new tablature. Remember, the thumb plays 6, 5, 4, 3, 2 and 1. The fingers brush down over the 4th, 3rd, 2nd and 1st strings whenever "D" is indicated. The brush-up is not used as yet.

G:

  6 , D , 6 , D , 5 , D , 5 , D , 4 , D , 4 , D , 3 , D , 3 , D , 2 , D , 2 , D , 1 ,

  D , 1 , D , 2 , D , 2 , D , 3 , D , 3 , D , 4 , D , 4 , D , 5 , D , 5 , D , 6 , D ,

  6 , D ,   etc.

When the fingers are brushing down properly with one solid sound coming forth, and when the thumb can pluck each string clearly, try the Carter Family Brush Style.

Rest the thumb on the 6th string as before and brush down with the fingers over the 4th, 3rd, 2nd and 1st strings. Now, brush UPWARD with the fingers. Do not pluck up with the fingers, but rather <u>drag</u> them, as a unit, up over the strings. The motion is similar to waving bye-bye (with the finger tips only) to a baby. The brush should drag up over the 1st, 2nd and 3rd strings. This up-brush should sound out as loudly as the down-brush. The entire motion should be controlled and small; do not use the whole hand in this motion, just the finger tips. The rhythm should be in your head, not in your hand or arm.

Practice brushing down and then up until both are smooth and clear, then try the Carter Family Brush Style itself.

The basic Carter Family Brush Style has four parts; a thumb-pluck on the bass string, a PAUSE which takes one equal count, a brush-down and (4) a brush-up.

```
6 ,   p a u s e ,   d o w n ,   u p
1         2           3         4
```

Again, each part of the right hand pattern gets an equal beat. This is very important. As you practice, tap your foot to insure that you maintain the steady rhythm. Say the words, "fried po-ta-toes," to remind yourself of the Carter Family Brush Style's rhythm.

```
6 ,   p a u s e ,   d o w n ,   u p
1         2           3         4
fried    po-          ta-      toes
```

The style must keep rolling with no breaks or pauses <u>except</u> after the thumb.

Here are several patterns which are variations on the basic 4-part Carter Family Brush Style:

2/4 and 4/4 Time Brush Styles

```
T , down
T , down , down , down
T , up , down , up
```

3/4 and 6/8 Time Brush Styles

```
T , down , down
T , pause , down , up , down , up
T , up , down , up , down , up
```

Try these brush styles with the songs given earlier in this manual. Due to the fast moving, rolling pattern of some of the above brush styles, you might have to play eight parts (T, pause, D, U, T, pause, D, U - for example) in place of the 4-part plucking styles you used before.

Maybelle Carter of the Carter Family uses only her index finger for the brush-down, brush-up. Her remaining fingers rest on the face of the guitar for support. This gives a brasher sound which is not adaptable to all folk songs. See which way of brushing you like the best.

REMEMBER: All the previous techniques, such as hammering-on, can be used with the brush styles. In fact, even plucking styles themselves can be combined with brush styles in order to gain interesting right hand patterns. It will take a solid right hand on your part to brush and pluck in one style, but try the following example for practice:

(A) Pluck a bass string with the thumb.

(B) Brush down over the treble strings.

(C) Pluck a bass string with the thumb.

(D) Pluck the treble strings (3, 2, 1) in three quick, separate notes.

TIMING FOR THIS PATTERN:

6,	D,	5,	I,M,R
1	2	3	4

As you can see, the first three parts fall right on the beat. In the last part, the index finger plucks slightly before the 4th beat; the middle finger plucks right on the beat; and the ring finger plucks slightly after the beat. The 1,2,3,4 foot tap must be even.

EXPERIMENTING WITH RIGHT HAND STYLES

All the right hand styles you have learned so far can be changed by experimentation. First of all, establish a basic right hand pattern for a song, "T,I,M,R," for example. Naturally, this 4-part right hand style will repeat itself as the song progresses, "T,I,M,R,T,I,M,R,T,I,M,R," etc. Now, instead of thinking in terms of groups 4-parts in length, think in terms of groups 8-parts in length. In other words,

in place of   "T,I,M,R,T,I,M,R" (4 parts played twice)

you could play   "T,I,M,R,M,I,M,R" (8 parts played once).

Instead of thinking in terms of groups 6-parts in length, think in terms of groups 12-parts in length.

In place of   "T,I,M,R,M,I,T,I,M,R,M,I" (6 parts played twice)

play   "T,I,M,R,M,I,M,R,M,I,M,R" (12 parts played once).

In the preceding examples, the right hand styles have been extended by the addition of ideas and parts characteristic of the original pattern. Perhaps a simpler way to think in terms of larger-numbered groups, is to combine two or more right hand patterns.

In place of   "T,IMR,IMR,T,IMR,IMR," (3 parts played twice)

play   "T,IMR,IMR,T,I,MR" (6 parts played once)

or   "T,IMR,IMR,T,pause,IMR" (6 parts played once).

(You may choose to combine completely different right hand styles.)

In place of   "T,I,M,R,T,I,M,R" (4 parts played twice)

play   "T,I,M,R,T,D,T,D" (8 parts played once)

or   "T,I,M,R,T,pause,D,U" (8 parts played once).

Another way to change right hand styles, is to pluck differently with the thumb. Instead of only plucking one bass string at a time, or simply alternating the order in which the bass strings are plucked, try plucking "654" in quick succession for one beat. The three strings should sound out as one unit. Try, "654,I,M,R" or "654,pause,D,U."

You may even experiment with plucking separate bass strings (with the thumb, of course) throughout the right hand patterns, such as: "6,5,4,IMR" (4 parts) or "6,5,4,I,M,R" (6 parts).

The fingers of the right hand may also pluck the "incorrect" strings!
For example, use the index finger for plucking the 2nd string, and the
middle finger for plucking the 1st string (the ring finger rests on the face
of the instrument for support). The thumb plays 6,5,4 and 3. With the
fingers placed in this manner, try, "4,I,M,3,I,M,4,I" (8 equal parts).
Experiment with this pattern for use in songs where an extra fast, rip-
ling accompaniment is needed.

In the above pattern there are eight parts, divided as follows:
"$\frac{4,I,M,3,I,M,4,I.}{1,2,3-1,2,3-1,2}$" Now, try changing the order of the pattern to
"1,2,3-1,2-1,2,3" or "1,2-1,2,3-1,2,3." Try plucking different bass
strings for other effects.

Two other techniques that you can add to right hand patterns,
are hammering-on whole chords and damping with the left hand.

Hammering-on whole chords is best used when several strings
are plucked or brushed at the same time. Simply lift the fretting fingers
off the strings just before you brush down; brush down and then forcefully
return the fingers to the proper chording position, as with a normal one-
string hammer-on. The more strings brushed or plucked, the greater the
effect. Also, the more fingers used in chording, the more the hammer-on
will sound out. For instance, in a barred chord try "654,D," hammering-on

the whole chord on the thumb beat ("654") and then again on the "D" beat. Experiment!

Damping with the left hand is excellent for creating a bouncing rhythm in brush styles. It is an off-beat muting of the strings. First, finger an A chord without actually pushing down on the strings to fret them. If you brush over the treble strings at this point you will get a dull "thud" sound. Now, brush across the treble strings and at the same time push down on the strings to fret the chord. As soon as the brush down is completed, keep the fingers touching the strings in the chord but again remove the fretting pressure. Removing the fretting pressure will "dampen" the sound of the chord. Now, try the right hand pattern "T, D, T, D." Keep the chording pressure relaxed during the thumb pluck and as you brush down, fret normally with full left hand pressure, being certain to relax the pressure the moment the brush down is completed. Although the beats and parts of the right hand style are counted the same, the effect is heavily rhythmic. Again, as with the full-chord hammer-on, this technique works best in chords where there is a maximum of fretted strings, such as in the barred chords.

COPYING RIGHT HAND ACCOMPANIMENT
PATTERNS FROM RECORDS

An excellent way to discover new right hand patterns is to copy what a performer is doing on record. This is actually quite easy to do, for all complex-sounding right hand accompaniment patterns you've been hearing on record are just combinations of the patterns you have already learned. Just keep in mind that although some of the patterns are difficult to hear while the performer is singing, the performer usually plays the same pattern between verses and at the beginning and end of the song, where no singing is done.

The first thing to do is to discover what <u>type</u> of right hand pattern is being used (be certain there is only one guitar on the record). Is it a brush style or a plucking style? If it is a brush style it will probably be related to the Carter Family Brush Style pattern. If the pattern seems too fast to discover which part is which, simply slow the record down to

1/2 speed and you will probably hear the familiar "T,pause,D,U" or a variant.

Plucking styles are a bit harder to figure out, but still they should cause you little difficulty if you have a good ear. Simply keep in mind that most plucking styles begin with a thumb pluck. This will be the lowest tone you hear. The index usually plucks the 3rd string; middle, the 2nd; and ring, the 1st string. So, if you hear, "lowest, higher, higher-yet, highest," the pattern is probably "T,I,M,R." "Lowest, high, not-so-high, a bit lower," the pattern is probably "T,R,M,I."

Be sure to listen for hammering-on and other techniques you have learned.

Work with records as much as possible. This will help you to develope a style of your own.

EVEN MORE SONGS

Here are some more songs. Try now to use

both the plucking and brush styles that you have learned.

Also, try the hammer-on. If the songs are not in the right key for

you, use the capo or transpose to another key.

By now, your hand should be rock-solid

with just the fingers moving when you

pluck. If this is so, you can remove

your little finger from the guitar face;

but make sure that your hand remains

unmoving as you pluck.

If you find it hard to use the brush styles, practice on the Chord Changing

Charts, pages 46 and 47.

BARBARA ALLEN

Joan Baez, Joan Baez, Vol. 2, (Vanguard Records) VRS-9094.
Burl Ives, Women, (Decca Records) DL-5490.
Pete Seeger, The Bitter and The Sweet, (Columbia Records) CL-1916.
Jean Ritchie, British Traditional Ballads in the Southern Mountains,
(Folkways Records) FA-2301.

(4/4 time)

```
T,     I,   M,   R,   T,I,M,R,T,I,      M,R,      T,I,M,R,T,
C                      G7                         C
    In  Scarlet  Town         where  I  was  born,

                       D7          G
    there  was  a  fair  maid  dwellin',

              F                   C
    made  every  youth  cry, well  a  day,

                       G7         C
    and  her  name  was  Barbara  Allen.
```

(2) All in the merry month of May,
    the green buds, they were swellin',
    Sweet William on his death bed lay
    all in love with Barbara Allen.

(3) He sent a servant to her door,
    to the place where she was dwellin',
    "O Miss, O Miss, O come you up,
    if your name be Barbara Allen."

(4) O slowly, slowly she got up,
    and slowly she came nigh him;
    and said so coldly unto him
    "Young man, I think you're dyin'."

NOTE: The right hand styles given with these songs are only suggestions.
Play each song in more than one style.

116

I KNOW WHERE I'M GOIN'

Odetta, <u>My Eyes Have Seen</u>, (Vanguard Records) VRS-9059.
Burl Ives, <u>Wayfaring Stranger</u>, (Columbia Records) CL-628.
The Weavers, <u>Folk Songs Around the World</u>, (Decca Records) DL-8909.

(2/4 time)

```
T,  IMR,  T,      IMR,T,    IMR,T,IMR,T,IMR,  T,
G
I  know  where  I'm  goin',       and  I  know  who's


IMR,   T,          IMR,T,IMR,
       D7
goin'  with me;


G                     G7                  C
I  know  who  I  love,  but  the  devil  knows  who


       D7
I'll  marry.
```

(2) I have stockings of silk, and shoes of fine green leather;
    combs to buckle my hair, and a ring for every finger.

(3) Feather beds are soft, and painted rooms are bonny,
    but I would give them all for my handsome, winsome Johnny.

(4) Some say he's black, but I say he's bonny;
    fairest of them all is my handsome, winsome Johnny.

NOTE: If you wish to use a 4-part right hand style for this song, you will
of course play the first two parts, say "T,I," where the "T" now stands.
The final two parts, say "M,R," should be played where the "IMR" is
found:
```
        T,I, M,R,   T,I, M,R,
        G                            and etc.
         I  know  where  I'm
```

117

ST. JAMES INFIRMARY

Pete Seeger, <u>American Favorite Ballads</u>, <u>Vol. 5</u>., (Folkways Records)
FA-2445.
Josh White, <u>Josh at Midnight</u>, (Elektra Records) EKL-102.

(4/4 time)

```
T,  I,  M,  R,     T,I,M,  R,  T,I,  M,R,  T,  I     M,R,T,I,
Am                          E7            Am
     It   was   down    in   old   Joe's   barroom


                         E7
on   a   corner   by   the   square;


             Am        E7            Am
they   were   serving   drinks   as   usual,


                  E7               Am
and   the   usual   crowd   was   there.
```


(2) On my left stood big Joe McKennedy,
    and his eyes were bloodshot red;
    he turned right to the people,
    and this is what he said:

(3) "Went down to St. James Infirmary,
    to see my baby there,
    she was stretched out on a long white table,
    so cool, so sweet, so fair."

(CHORUS) "Let her go, let her go, God bless her,
          wherever she may be;
          she can search the whole world over,
          and never find a Sweet Man like me."

WAYFARING STRANGER

Bill Monroe, Country Jubilee, (Decca Records) DL-4172.
Pete Seeger, Frontier Ballads, Vol. 2, (Folkways Records) FA-2176.
Bob Gibson & Bob Camp, At the Gate of Horn, (Elektra Records) EKS 7-207.

(4/4 time)

```
T,  I,   MR,  I,
T,  R,   M,   I,      (three suggested right hand styles )
T,  I,   M,   R,
Em                        B7           Em
    I'm  just  a  poor      wayfaring   stranger.


              Am                        B7
a-trav'ling  through  this  world  of  woe.


              Em
But there's  no  sickness,  toil  or  trouble,


              A   Am      to  which  I  go.
in that fair land


                              Am
I'm going  there  to  see  my  mother,


              C    D         G
I'm going  there    no  more  to  roam.


              B7          Em
I m just a-go - ing  over  Jordan,


              A  Am               Em
I'm just a-go -  ing   over   home.
```

THE DRUNKEN SAILOR

Pete Seeger, <u>American Favorite Ballads</u>, <u>Vol. 4</u>, (Folkways Records) FA-2323.
Burl Ives, <u>Down to the Sea in Ships</u>, (Decca Records) DL-8245.

(2/4 time)

```
T,    U, D, U, T,U,D,   U,T,U,D,U, T,U,D,U,
Am
What ya gonna do  with a drunken  sailor,


G
what ya gonna do with a drunken  sailor,


Am
what ya gonna do with a drunken  sailor,


G            Am
early in the mornin'?
```

(CHORUS)

```
AM
Hoo-ray, up she rises,

G
Hoo-ray, and up she rises,

Am
Hooray, and up she rises,

G    E7    Am
Early in the mornin'.
```

(2) Put him in the long-boat 'til he's sober. (Similarly)
(3) Shave his belly with a rusty razor.
(4) Don't give him any chocolate ice cream.
(5) That's what you do with a drunken sailor.

WHEN THE
SAINTS GO MARCHIN' IN

The Weavers, The Best of the Weavers, (Decca Records) DL-8893.
Lightnin' Hopkins, Autobiography in Blues, (Tradition Records) TLP-1040.
The Kingston Trio, ...from the "Hungry i," (Capitol Records) T-1107.

(2/4 time)
-three suggested right hand styles-

```
T,        D,      T, D, T, D, T,    D,  T, D,    T,D,T,D,T,D,
T,        IMR,    T, IMR, T, IMR, T,    IMR, T, IMR,  etc.
T,pause, D,U,    T,p,D,U,T,p,D,U,T,p,  D,U,  T,p,D,U,  etc.
D
When     the   Saints              go   marchin' in,
```

```
                                          A7
when    the   Saints   go   marchin'  in,
```

```
              D                            G
Lord,    I   want   to   be   in   that   number,
```

```
              D         A7         D
when    the   Saints   go   marchin'   in.
```

(2) When the sun refuse to shine,
    when the sun refuse to shine,
    Lord, I want to be in that number,
    when the sun refuse to shine.

(3) When the new world is revealed. (similarly)

(4) When the moon has turned to blood.

(5) When the Master, He has come.

(6) When the Revelation comes.

(7) When the Saints go marchin' in.

BASS STRING RUNS

A professional-sounding embellishment to any folksong is the addition of BASS STRING RUNS. Bass string runs are groups of single bass notes which take the place of normal right hand patterns. A run does not make a folksong longer or shorter. Rather, a complete right hand pattern is taken out of the song and a run put in its place. There is no loss of rhythm or momentum when a run is used, instead, a definite stable series of single notes is introduced to lend interest and color to the comparative monotony of continuous right hand patterns.

Runs may be played as introductions and endings to songs, or more commonly, during the song to join chords. To play a run while singing takes complete mastery of run techniques, so I suggest practicing the runs without singing until you develop an ear for their use.

One run in each key is sufficient. Don't try to play a completely different run every time. Many performers use only two or three runs for hundreds of songs. And, like anything else, too much of a good thing becomes boring.

READ THE FOLLOWING MATERIAL CAREFULLY AND PLAY THE
EXAMPLES EXTRA SLOWLY!

Now that you have mastered a 3/4 time plucking style (such as "T,IMR,IMR") and can keep it going dump-di-di, dump-di-di, through several chord changes and three-chord groups, you will be able to try the following run.

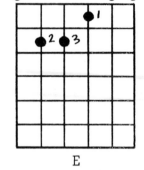

E

First, try the series below in an E chord: The thumb plucks only the bass string tonic note (6th string), as noted.

E
 6,   IMR,   IMR,   6,   IMR,   IMR,   6,   IMR,   IMR.
 /   /   /
dump - di - di, dump - di - di, dump - di - di .

Now, take one of the 3-part right hand patterns out of the series and in its place tap your foot. To maintain rhythm tap your foot heavily on the emphasis marks.

E
 6,   IMR,   IMR,   tap,   tap,   tap,   6,   IMR,   IMR.
 /   /   /
dump - di - di, dump - di - di, dump - di - di .

The actual run on the bass strings will take the place of the omitted right hand pattern, so try the above series several times until you can easily stop the right hand pattern and interject the foot taps on the beat.

The notes of the run are diagrammed in the chord boxes below (I, II, III). An "o" above a string means to pluck the string open or unfretted. When the other chord boxes are called for, fret only where indicated. The diagrams are not of complete chords; but of places to fret the string being plucked. To finger the run you will have to remove your fingers from the E chord.

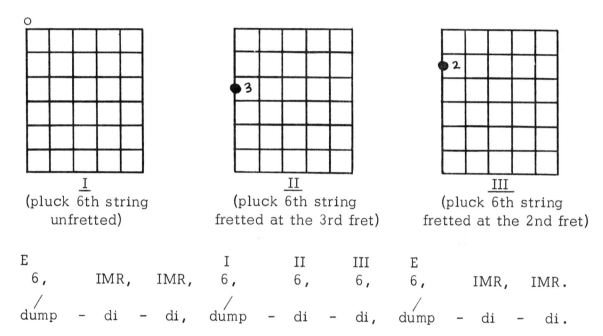

I	II	III
(pluck 6th string unfretted)	(pluck 6th string fretted at the 3rd fret)	(pluck 6th string fretted at the 2nd fret)

```
E                        I     II    III   E
6,     IMR,   IMR,   6,    6,    6,    6,     IMR,   IMR.
 /                    /                 /
dump - di - di,   dump - di - di,   dump - di - di.
```

Be certain that there is no loss in rhythm when the run ends and the chord is fingered again. The run itself should maintain the solid dump-di-di rhythm with no breaks of any kind before, during or after the run.

As you can see, the run has simply taken the place of the right hand pattern left out of the series. Also notice the "6, IMR, IMR" directly following the run. The "6" (tonic bass string of the E chord), although

it is part of the right hand pattern, is actually a note of the run, the fourth
note of the run.

```
               I   II  III  E
E
6,  IMR,  IMR,  6,   6,   6,   6,   IMR,  IMR.
                  entire run
```

All the rules for constructing bass note runs will be reviewed later
in this section, but for now, memorize the following

RULE: A run has the same number of parts as the right hand style it re-
placed plus one. The plus one is the thumb pluck of the right hand
pattern directly following the run itself.

RULE: The last, "plus one," note of a run is the tonic bass string of the
chord directly following the run itself.

To correctly execute the fingering of the previous run, be certain
that the strings are fretted with separate fingers. Do not slide fingers
from one fret to another when executing a run. Simply reach the fingers
to the appropriate fret as illustrated on the opposite page.

125

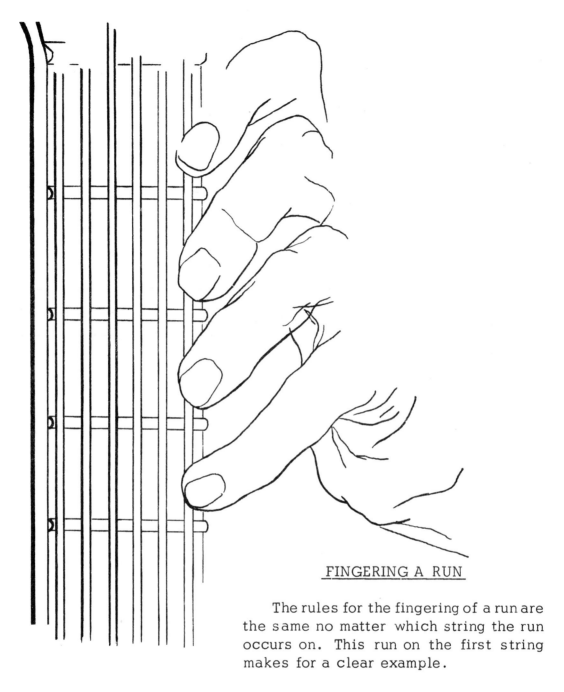

FINGERING A RUN

The rules for the fingering of a run are the same no matter which string the run occurs on. This run on the first string makes for a clear example.

The index finger of the chording hand is fretting at the first fret of the run, the middle finger at the second, ring finger at the third and little finger at the fourth fret of the run.

If the note at the third fret was called for, the little finger would be removed, etc. If a note at the fifth fret was called for, the index finger would fret it. <u>The little finger would not slide up</u>. <u>Different fingers are used for each consecutive note of a run</u>.

Here is a run similar to the first except that it is in a 4-part right hand style. The E chord will be used again. How many parts will the run have? What will be the last note plucked in the run? See the preceding rules to refresh your memory.

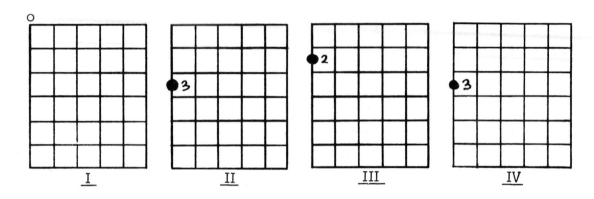

```
E                          I     II   III  IV   E
  6,    I,   M,   R,   6,    6,   6,   6,   6,    I,   M,   R .
  /                        /                  /
dump - di - di - di,  dump - di - di - di,  dump - di - di - di.
```

As with the run in the 3-part right hand pattern, the last note of the run is actually the first note of the right hand pattern directly following the run itself. The right hand pattern has four parts so the run itself has the same number of parts (falling on the original right hand pattern's beats) PLUS ONE. The "plus one" is, again, the "6" of the "6,I,M,R" directly following the run itself.

So far you have learned how to take out a right hand pattern and put a run in its place. You have only done this while staying in a single chord.

Usually runs are used to <u>join</u> one chord to another. This is a bit more difficult and should only be tried when you are confident about chord changing. You don't want to loose the rhythm and destroy the momentum of the run just because of a faulty chord change.

Before going over all the rules concerning run construction, try connecting two chords with a run. You will be using the E chord and an A chord:

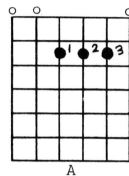

A

In this example you will not be using special fingering for the run as before, but rather you will pluck strings <u>already</u> <u>fretted</u> <u>within</u> <u>the</u> <u>E</u> <u>chord</u> as the notes of the run. Keep the hand <u>on</u> <u>the</u> <u>chord</u> until the chord change to A is indicated.

E   <u>A</u>

6,   IMR, IMR, 6,   IMR, IMR, 6,   5,   4,   5,   IMR,IMR.

dump - di - di, dump - di - di, dump - di - di, dump - di - di.

The actual run is done while in the E chord. Simply pluck the 6th, 5th and then the 4th strings in rhythm with the thumb, change to the A chord and pluck the 5th string (bass string tonic note) for the last note of the run.

Important Rules For Creating Your Own Runs

(1)   A run has the same number of parts as the right hand style it replaces plus one. If the run seems to drag, double the number of parts (instead of 2 plus one, play 4 plus one). If the right hand style has too many parts and the run is impossible to play part-for-part at that speed, cut the number of parts in half (instead of 4 plus one, 2 plus one). But, double or halved the notes of the run take the same amount of time as the pattern they replace, plus one (see pg. 133).

(2)   It is best to play runs only on the 6th, 5th and 4th strings (bass string runs) until you become proficient. But, if you must play some of the notes of a run on the treble strings, for the time being use your thumb to pluck them.

(3)   The very last note of a run (the "plus one" note) should be the bass string tonic note of the chord you are running to. For example, if you are joining a C chord to a G chord (the G chord being the chord you are running to) the last note of the run should be G. If you are running from an A chord to an E chord the last note of the run should be E.

(4)   The first note of the run can be practically any note at all, but it is best for beginners to play the tonic note of the chord they are running from. Therefore a run from an A chord to an E chord should

begin with the note A (5th string open) and end with the note E (6th string open).

(5)   The notes between the first and last note may be any notes that sound good to you. They may ascend in tone, descend in tone, or do both. Anything that sounds good to your ear is permissible.

(6)   Every other note of the run should be different.

On the following pages there are some more runs. They are all to be played "within the chord," that is, <u>you</u> <u>do not</u> <u>have to</u> <u>remove your fingers from the chord you are in,</u> in order to play the run. The only exception to this rule occurs where you find the word "open." Directly following a string, this word signifies that the string is to be plucked unfretted. You must remove the fretting finger from the string. The remainder of the chord stays intact. The removed finger is returned after the open string has been played. Many times the very next note will require that the entire chord is intact.

 Directions for playing these runs are found on the preceding page.

(2-part right hand styles)

E
6, IMR, 6, IMR, 4, 5, 5, IMR, 5, IMR.
          A

E
6, IMR, 6, IMR, 5(open), 5, 5, IMR, 5, IMR.
           A

E
6, IMR, 6, IMR, 4(open), 4, 5, IMR, 5, IMR.
           A

G
6, IMR, 6, IMR, 5(open), 5, 5, IMR, 5, IMR.
           C

G
6, IMR, 6, IMR, 4, 5, 5, IMR, 5, IMR.
          C

A
5, IMR, 5, IMR, 4(open), 4, 4, IMR, 4, IMR.
           D

A
5, IMR, 5, IMR, 4, 5, 4, IMR, 4, IMR.
          D

(3-part right hand styles)

E
6, IMR, IMR, 6, IMR, IMR, 6, 5(open), 5, 5, IMR, IMR.
               A

E
6, IMR, IMR, 6, IMR, IMR, 5(open), 5, 4, 5, IMR, IMR.
               A

```
G                                          C
6, IMR, IMR, 6, IMR, IMR, 5(open), 5, 4, 5, IMR, IMR.


G                                        C
6, IMR, IMR, 6, IMR, IMR, 5, 4, 5, 5, IMR, IMR.


A                                                   D
5, IMR, IMR, 5, IMR, IMR, 4, 4(open), 4, 4, IMR, IMR.


A                                               D
5, IMR, IMR. 5, IMR, IMR, 4, 5, 4, 4, IMR, IMR.



                    (4-part right hand styles)


E                                               A
6, I, M, R, 6, I, M, R, 6, 5(open), 5, 4, 5, I, M, R, 5, I, M, R.


E                                               A
6, I, M, R, 6, I, M, R, 5(open), 5, 4(open), 4, 5, I, M, R, 5, I, M, R.


G                                                   C
6, I, M, R, 6, I, M, R, 6, 5(open), 5, 4, 5, I, M, R, 5, I, M, R.


G                                               C
6, I, M, R, 6, I, M, R, 5, 5(open), 5, 4, 5, I, M, R, 5, I, M, R.


A                                               D
5, I, M, R, 5, I, M, R, 5, 4(open), 4, 5, 4, I, M, R, 4, I, M, R.


A                                       D
5, I, M, R, 5, I, M, R, 5, 4, 5, 4, 4, I, M, R, 4, I, M, R.
```

Runs In Carter Family Brush Style

Since the Carter Family Brush Style is made up of four parts (T , pause , D , U ,), a run in this style should have four parts plus one.

G   C
6,pause,D,U,6,pause,D,U,6,6(open),6,5,5,pause,D,U,5,pause,D,U.

You probably found the above run difficult to do because the Carter Family Brush Style is usually played quickly, making the run hurried. This is a problem that arises whenever a run is used within a right hand pattern that is played rapidly.

Whenever a run cannot be comfortably placed in a pattern due to the speed required, simply cut the number of parts of the run in half and give each part twice its normal beat. When placing a run within a Carter Family right hand pattern, instead of four plus one, play two plus one. (See Rule #1, page 129.)

G   C
6,pause,D,U,6,pause,D,U, 6, 5, 5,pause,D,U,5,pause,D,U.

G   C
6,pause,D,U,6,pause,D,U, 5(open), 5, 5,pause,D,U,5,pause,D,U.

INSTRUMENTAL MELODY STYLES
and...FINGER-PICKING AS ACCOMPANIMENT

Here is an introduction to melody-playing and instrumental techniques. Look for more extensive coverage of important folk instrumental styles in BAXTER'S INTERMEDIATE GUITAR MANUALS.

As you now know, the notes on each string progress by half-steps one fret at a time. These notes also appear on the music staff. It would seem a simple matter to remember notes on the staff and play the melody as given. However, the notes on the staff in folksong books are usually simple melody lines for one-note-at-a-time piano playing. This is unsuitable for guitar playing because all good folk instrumental styles incorporate full chord patterns involving several notes at the same time.

So, again you must turn to tablature; but you will find very little tablature for the important folk instrumental styles because most of this music is learned and passed on by ear. You see, the writers and creators of folk instrumental music are not composers who work with a pencil and paper in front of their guitar, but the performers themselves. Whether they perform for hundreds, family or just their own ears, most often they have no need to write down what they play. These people do not worry about repeating a piece note for note. Perhaps the next time they play the song it will be even better!

Now perhaps you can see why this manual and the others to follow try so hard to give you a solid foundation so that you will learn, not a number of songs, but learn, instead, how to play any song whether you find it in a song book, hear it sung by a friend, hear it on record or whatever.

The songs in this section will present three basic ways of playing melody. It is the styles and techniques that are important, not the songs themselves. Indeed, I do not advise that you study the first song past "being able to hear how the melody is plucked and backed up with the thumb and brush." The song and style are simple and presented merely to introduce you to this new sound. Practice this first song only until you are able to concentrate on melody part and rhythm part at the same time. Then, it should be no trouble for you to play the melody of the songs found earlier in this manual.

There is a time and place for what you are about to learn. Most often, this is at the start, finish and between verses. Playing melody while you sing may distract from the words. Most performers continue the right hand instrumental style during verses but they pluck other than the melody strings or they pluck a simple accompaniment version of the melody style.

(I.) <u>T r e b l e   S t r i n g   M e l o d y   A g a i n s t   A   C o n s t a n t   B a s s</u> :

(A) <u>The thumb plucks down on a bass string and at the same time</u>
     <u>the index finger plucks up on the appropriate treble string.</u>
     <u>This is one beat</u>.

     For example, the thumb plucks the 5th string and the index

     finger plucks the 1st string at the same time. This would be

     notated: "51." In the tablature used to present this style of

     music it is impossible to say that the index finger will pluck

     only a certain string while the middle finger plucks another,

     etc., so "I, M, R" can no longer be used in the tablature.

     Instead, the treble string that is to be plucked is noted, and

     in most cases you can pluck this string with either the index

     or the middle finger.

(B) <u>The fingers brush down across the 4th, 3rd, 2nd and 1st</u>
     <u>strings for the second beat</u>. Both beats are equal in length.
     The brush down is notated: "D."

The rhythm of this first instrumental style is $\overset{/}{1}$,2,$\overset{/}{1}$,2,$\overset{/}{1}$,2. In step A the

index finger plucks the melody while the thumb adds fullness to the song.

The index or middle finger pluck could be left out of this step if the melody

demanded. The thumb would pluck by itself to retain the rhythm.

SKIP TO MY LOU

Pete Seeger, American Favorite Ballads, Vol. 1, (Folkways Records) FA-2320.
Jean Ritchie, Jean Ritchie Sings, (Elektra Records) EKL-125.

(2/4 time)

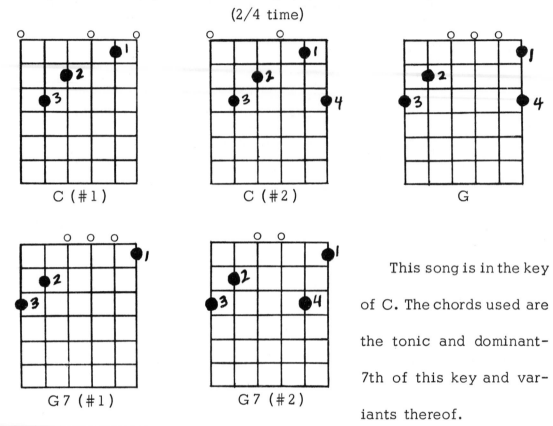

C (#1)   C (#2)   G

G 7 (#1)   G 7 (#2)

This song is in the key of C. The chords used are the tonic and dominant-7th of this key and variants thereof.

This song employs the instrumental style you learned on the preceding page, "Treble String Melody Against A Constant Bass." Each part of the right hand style receives an equal beat: 1,2,1,2,1,2. "D," of course means that the fingers brush down. As always, the numbers in the tablature refer to the strings. "51," means that the 5th and 1st strings are to be sounded together. The thumb plucks the 6th, 5th and 4th strings. The 1st, 2nd and 3rd strings are plucked by either the index or middle fingers. I suggest bracing the ring finger on the face of the guitar.

In the second to the last line, "62,41,61(open),42," all the beats are played, "thumb-and-index at the same time." The "41" and the "42" take the place of the usual "D." "61(open)" means that the 6th string is plucked as fretted within the chord, but that the 1st string is to be plucked unfretted or open.

Skip To My Lou

```
                      Lou,      Lou,      skip to my
Form  C(#1): and play 51,   D,  42,  D,  51,  D,

                      Lou.
change to C(#2): play 51,  D,

                 Lou,
      G7(#2):    62,  D,

                 Lou,
      G7(#1):    42,  D,

                 skip  to my
      G7(#2):    62,  D,

                 Lou.
         G:      51,  D,

                 Lou,      Lou,      skip to my
      C(#1):     51,  D,   42,  D,   51,  D,

                 Lou.
      C(#2):     51,  D,

                 Skip  to my   Lou,      my
      G7(#2):    62,   41,  61(open),  42,

                 Dar-        ling.
      C(#1):     42,  D,  42 .
```

(II.) <u>Carter Family Brush Style Melody</u>:

(You can review the Carter Family Brush Style on page 106.)

In the following piece the numbers 6,5,4,3,2 and 1 = the strings to be plucked by the thumb. "P" = pause, "D" = down brush and "U" = up brush.

"6(open)" or "6(o)" = pluck the 6th string unfretted or open.

"4(2)" = pluck the 4th string fretted at the second fret. The parenthesis implies that the 4th string either was not fretted in the chord you are in or that it was fretted somewhere other than at the 4th fret. The 4th string, 2nd fret note is needed for the melody and so the parenthesis is used. When fretting for such a melody note, the rest of the chord should remain intact; only the nearest finger should move to fret the string. The fretting finger is returned to its original position for the next beat. Parenthesis numbers always stand for fret numbers. Thus, "5(2)" = pluck the 5th string fretted at the 2nd fret.

A hammer-on is noted, "(H)." "6(H)" = pluck the 6th string and where it is normally fretted within the chord hammer-on. "6(H2)" = pluck the 6th string and hammer-on at the 2nd fret. Normally, this type of hammer-on, one that is not within a chord, takes place on an open string. Use the nearest finger for the hammer-on. If the 6th string was already fretted at the 1st fret, the fretting finger would not be removed. Another finger would perform the hammer-on at the 2nd fret. You can review the hammer-on on page 91.

In this piece you will also find, "5 , p , 4 , p , " etc. These 4 beats take the place of one 4-beat Carter Family Brush pattern. No change in rhythm should result from the substitution. It is simply a way of gaining the melody.

In order to present "JESSE JAMES" on two facing pages, the discography will be given now.

JESSE JAMES

Pete Seeger, American Ballads, (Folkways Records) FA-2319.
Ed McCurdy, Songs of the Old West, (Elektra Records) EKL-112.

(2/4 time)

JESSE JAMES

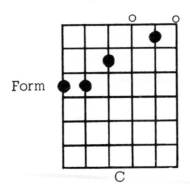

Form   C

and
play: 5 , p , 4(o) , p , 4(H) , p , D , U , 4 , p ,
    Jes - se   James   was

4(o) , p , 5 , p , D , U , 6 , p , D , U ,
a   Lad   who

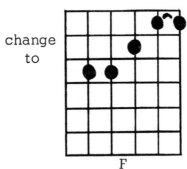

change
to   F

and
play: 5(o) , p , D , U , 5 , p , 5(o) , p ,
    killed   many   a

back to   C   and play: 6 , p , D , U , 5 , p , 4(o) , p , 4(H) , p , D , U ,
                man.   He   robbed

4 , p , D , U , 3 , p , D , U , 4 , p , D , U ,
the   Glen - dale

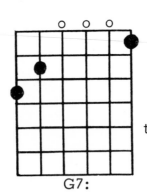

G7:

4 , p , D , U , 5 , p , D , U , 4 , p , D , U , 5 , p , 4 , p ,
train.   He

C: 4 , p , D , U , 4 , p , 4(o) , p , 5 , p , D , U , 6 , p , 6 , p ,
     stole   from   rich   and   he

F: 5(o) , p , D , U , 5 , p , 5(o) , p ,
    gave   to   the

C:

    6 , p , D , U , 5 , p , 4(o) , p , 4(H) , p , D , U , 4 , p , 4 , p ,
poor,   he'd   a   hand   and   a

G7:

    4 , p , D , U , 4(2) , p , 4 , p ,
heart   and   a

C:

    5 , p , D , U , 6 , p , 5(2) , p , 5 , p , D , U , 4 , p , D , U , 5 , p , 5 , p , 4(o) , p , 4 , p ,
brain.

(CHORUS)

F:

    4 , p , D , U , 4 , p , 4 , p , 4 , p , D , U , 4 , p , D , U ,
Jes - se   had   a   wife   who

C:

    4 , p , D , U , 4 , p , 4(o) , p , 5 , p , D , U , 5 , p , 4 , p , 3 , p , D , U ,
mourned   for   his   life,   three   chil -

        3 , p , D , U , 3 , p , D , U , 4 , p , D , U ,
    dren   they   were

G7:

    4 , p , D , U , 6 , p , 5 , p , 4 , p , D , U , 5 , p , 4 , p ,
brave,   but that

C:

    4 , p , D , U , 4 , p , 4(o) , p , 5 , p , D , U , 6 , p , 6 , p ,
dir - ty lit - tle coward   that

F:

    5(o) , p , D , U , 5 , p , 5(o) , p ,
shot   mis - ter

C:

    6 , p , D , U , 5 , p , 4(o) , p , 4(H) , p , D , U , 4 , p , D , U ,
Howard   has   laid   poor

G7:

    4 , p , D , U , 4(2) , p , 4 , p ,
Jes - se   in   his

C:

   5 , p , D , U , 4 , p , D , U , 5 .
grave.

It was Robert Ford, that dirty little coward;

I wonder how he does feel,

For he ate of Jesse's bread, and he slept in Jesse's bed,

then he laid poor Jesse in his grave. (Chorus)

It was on a Saturday night, Jesse was at home,

talking with his family brave;

Robert Ford came along like a thief in the night

and laid poor Jesse in his grave. (Chorus)

The people held their breath when they heard of Jesse's death,

and wondered how he ever came to die;

It was one of the gang called little Robert Ford,

that shot poor Jesse on the sly. (Chorus)

This song was made by Billy Gashade,

as soon as the news did arrive;

He said there was no man with the law in his hand

that could take Jesse James when alive. (Chorus)

(III.) Arpeggio Style Melody:

The melody of a song is usually played in the same style in which you played the accompaniment. "Jesse James" is more properly played with a Carter Family Brush Style pattern. "Greensleeves" is properly played using an arpeggio style; whether you are accompanying your voice or playing the melody.

The tablature for this style again uses "6,5,4,I,M,R." The numbers refer to the bass strings which are always plucked by the thumb. "I," "M" and "R" refer to the index, middle and ring fingers. The index finger always plucks the 3rd string; the middle always plucks the 2nd; and the ring finger always plucks the 1st string.

In Arpeggio Style Melody the melody is usually played on the bass strings while the rhythm part is on the treble strings. In "Greensleeves" there is one exception to this rule. On the C-chord lines in the chorus the 3rd string takes the melody. So on these lines the index finger should be emphasized to insure that the melody rings out.

GREENSLEEVES

Susan Reed, <u>Susan Reed</u>, (Elektra Records) EKL-116.
Richard Dyer-Bennett, <u>Twentieth Century Minstrel</u>, (Decca Records)
DL-9102.
Cynthia Gooding and Theo Bikel, <u>Young Man and a Maid</u>, (Elektra
Records) EKS7-109.
The Weavers, <u>Folk Songs Around the World</u>, (Decca Records) DL-8909.

(6/8 time)

This is a comparitively easy melodic version of "Greensleeves."
The melody evolves from a "6 , I , M , R , M , I " pattern (6 parts), which
should be practiced before actually trying the piece in its entirety. Each
part of the pattern gets one equal beat, although there is a slight emphasis on the melody note.

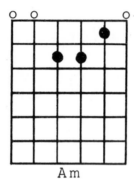

Am

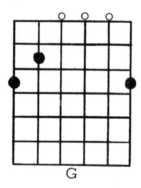

G

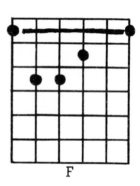

F

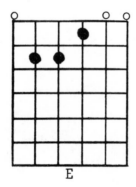

E

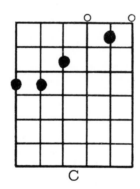

C

145

Greensleeves

Am:
```
   5,  I,  4,  I,  M,  R,  4,  I,  4,  I,  M,  R,  4,  I,
   A  -  las,         my      love,           you
```

G:
```
   4,  I,  M,  R,  5,  I,  6,  I,  M,  R,  6,  5,
   do          me    wrong               to
```

F:
```
   5,  I,  M,  R,  6,  I,  6,  I,  M,  R,  5,  I,
   cast        me      out            dis  -
```

E:
```
   5,  I,  M,  R,  6,  I,  6,  I,  M,  R,  M,  I,
   cour  -  teous  -  ly,                for
```

Am:
```
   4,  I,  M,  R,  4,  I,  4,  I,  M,  R,  4,  I,
   I          have  lov  -  ed you
```

G: F
```
   4,  I,  M,  R,  5,  I,  6,  I,  M,  R,  6,  5,  5,  I,  M,  R,  6,  5,
   O          so    long         de  light  -  ting
```

E: Am
```
   5,  I,  M,  R,  6,  5,  5,  I,  M,  R,  M,  I,  5 I M R,
   in          thy    com  -  pa  -  ny.
```

 (CHORUS)

146

C:
    I, M, R, M, I, M, I, M, R, M, I, 4,
Green   -   sleeves   was

G:
    4, I, M, R, 5, I, 6, I, M, R, 5, I,
    all   my   joy,

F:
    5, I, M, R, 6, I, 6, I, M, R, M, I,
Green   -   sleeves   was

E:
    5, I, M, R, M, I, 6, I, MR, I, MR, I,
    my   de - light,

C:
    I, M, R, M, I, M, I, M, R, M, I, 4,
Green   -   sleeves   was my

G:
    4, I, M, R, 5, I, 6, I, M, R, 5, I,
heart   of   gold,   and

F: E
    5, I, M, R, 5, 4, 5, I, M, R, M, I,
who   but my La   -   dy

Am:
    5, I, M, R, M, I, BRUSH DOWN.
Green   -   sleeves.

(IV.) Finger-Picking As Accompaniment:

Easily the most complex of the melody styles, Finger-Picking is a particular melody style akin to Traditional Blues. For a thorough understanding of Finger-Picking for playing melody, see BAXTER'S FINGER-PICKING MANUAL, however, here I will set down a few of the rules and give you several exercises with emphasis on using Finger-Picking for accompaniment.

Don't expect to master this style from these few short pages. For excellent examples of Finger-Picking listen to Elizabeth Cotten, Mississippi John Hurt, Etta Baker, Merle Travis and Doc Watson.

Although there are many possible variations, in theory, Finger-Picking goes like this: A melody is played on the treble strings (which are plucked separately or together). Behind the melody there is a constant-tempoed alternating bass string pattern called the "constantly-moving bass." The thumb is of course responsible for the alternating bass and the index finger will pluck the melody on the three treble strings. The ring and/or the middle finger rests on the face of the guitar for support.

Finger a C chord. Thumb-pluck first the 5th and then the 4th string in a 1-2,1-2,1-2, rhythm. Do not rest the thumb on the string below when plucking bass strings in this style.

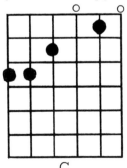

C

With the thumb plucking a constant $\overset{/}{5},\overset{/}{4},\overset{/}{5},\overset{/}{4},\overset{/}{5},\overset{/}{4}$ bass pattern, the index finger plucks the melody in two basic ways.

(A) The index finger can pluck the treble string melod$\overset{/}{y}$ <u>ON THE</u> <u>BEAT</u>. This results in a thumb-index "pinch," i.e., the index plucks a treble string at the same time as the thumb plucks the bass string. Tap your foot to sustain the proper rhythm.

Example #1: $\overset{/}{5}1,\overset{/}{4},\overset{/}{5}1,\overset{/}{4},\overset{/}{5}2,\overset{/}{4},\overset{/}{5}2,\overset{/}{4}$ The "5" of the "5,4"

bass is considered the first beat of the pattern. In this example the pinch comes only on the first beat.

Example #2: $\overset{/}{5}1,\overset{/}{4}2,\overset{/}{5}1,\overset{/}{4}2,\overset{/}{5}1,\overset{/}{4}2$ Here, there is a pinch on

both beats of the pattern.

(B) The second basic approach to Finger-Picking style is to play the melody <u>between</u> the beats of the constant bass. <u>Exactly</u> <u>between</u> <u>the</u> <u>beats</u>.

Example #3: $\overset{/}{5},1,\overset{/}{4},2,\overset{/}{5},1,\overset{/}{4},2,\overset{/}{5},1,\overset{/}{4}$ The thumb plucks

fall directly <u>on</u> the foot-tap emphasis, the treble notes coming directly <u>between</u> the bass string plucks.

Practice the above patterns (Examples #1, #2 and #3) until the "$\overset{/}{5},\overset{/}{4},\overset{/}{5},\overset{/}{4}$" follows a constant $\overset{/}{1}$-$\overset{/}{2},\overset{/}{1}$-$\overset{/}{2}$ rhythm with the treble notes falling either directly ON THE BEAT (the "pinch") or directly BETWEEN THE BEATS.

Finger-Picking is more commonly used for 4/4 and 2/4 time songs because in 3/4 or 6/8 time songs there can be no "constantly-moving" 1-2,1-2 bass string pattern. So the accompaniment Finger-Picking patterns which follow will be only for 4/4 and 2/4 time songs.

With the thumb playing 5,4,5,4 on the beat (emphasis marks denote foot-taps) and the index finger plucking the treble strings, carefully try these patterns. Be sure to tap your foot only on the emphasis marks. The patterns combine both on-beat and off-beat treble string plucking. Establish a constant foot-tap and do not let the addition or lack of a treble string pluck between the taps disturb this even rhythm.

C
chord: (1) 5,2,4,1,5,2,4,5,2,4,1,5,2,4,5,2,4,1,5,2,4, etc.

> This pattern, repeated three times, has a treble string pluck between each bass string pluck, except between the patterns themselves. Be careful not to loose the rhythm in these places.

(2) 5,2,4,51,2,4,5,2,4,51,2,4,5,2,4,51,2,4, etc.

(3) 5,2,41,5,2,4,5,2,41,5,2,4,5,2,41,5,2,4, etc.

You may combine the above patterns to form new patterns of your own. Just be sure that there are only four thumb beats per pattern, as above. When you use these patterns in other chords, the thumb should pluck the bass string tonic note of that chord. For chords where the tonic note falls on the 4th string (D, for example) play "5,4,5,4" as the bass line.

ARE YOU READY TO GO ON TO ANOTHER MANUAL? Usually a teacher would help you make this decision, but since you may be learning solely from this manual, mark the following check list "yes" or "no." If there are any "no's," it is best to go over the material in this manual until you have mastered all the techniques and concepts. You might be able to go on without mastering everything in this manual, but, because of a lack of understanding and ability, more advanced playing would sound mechanical and unprofessional in your hands. Be honest with yourself and continue on to a second manual only if you mark each statement "yes."

___ (1) Do you know how to transpose from one key to any other key, regardless of the number of chords involved?

___ (2) Can you barre a chord easily with no loss of rhythm?

___ (3) Can you construct any chord through use of the barre?

___ (4) Can you apply the rules outlined in this manual to songbooks?

___ (5) Can you easily accompany yourself in songs, without having to look at a book?

___ (6) Can you hammer-on and pull-off?

___ (7) Can you place a run in a song?

___ (8) Can you play the instrumental pieces without pausing and without the strings buzzing?

___ (9) Can you play any song easily in the keys of A, C, D, E and G?

___ (10) Can you use the capo for playing in any key you desire?

___ (11) Can you answer all the quizes in this manual correctly?

___ (12) Is your right hand solid and controlled in its movements?

If your answers are all "yes," you are no longer a beginning player. In fact, some might call you an advanced player, considering the material this book covers.

CHORDS

Here are all the chords you will need for folk accompaniment styles. Each chord is given in several positions up and down the guitar neck, although the most-used position appears at the top of each column. This is sort of a dictionary of chords, for the first page contains A major, A minor, A7th, A augmented and A diminished chords; and the next page contains B chords; and etc. This is not a list of three-chord groups. (After reading this manual you can figure these out for yourself.) To fully understand the chord diagrams themselves, see pages 14 and 34.

Although an unknown and seemingly precise chord may be called for in a song, all chords may be broken-down into five basic categories: Major Chords, Minor Chords, 7th Chords, and Augmented and Diminished Chords. Until you learn to construct chords other than the five basics (see BAXTER'S INTERMEDIATE MANUALS), use the following Substitution Chart so that you may play any song no matter what chords are called for.

CHORD SUBSTITUTION CHART
(USING AN "A" CHORD AS AN EXAMPLE)

For A, Aadd6, A6, Amaj7, or Amaj9 : <u>an A chord may be played</u>.

For Ami, Am, Ami7, Am7, Ami6, Am6, Am7-5, or Am7b5 : <u>an A minor</u>

<u>chord may be played</u>.

For A7th, A7, A9th, A9, A7-5, A7b5, A7aug, A7+, A7-9, A7+5, A-9,

A9b, A9-5, A+9, or A9(#5) : <u>an A seventh (dominant 7th) chord</u>

<u>may be played</u>.

Aaug, or A+ stands for "A augmented chord."

Adim7, Adim or A^O stands for "A diminished chord."

A major chords

A minor chords

A 7th chords

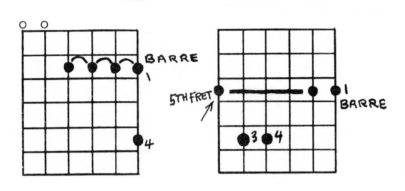

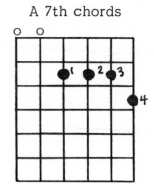

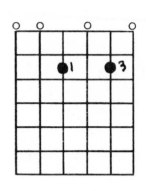

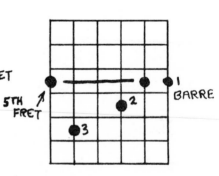

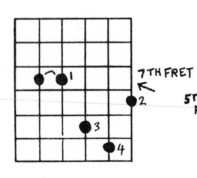

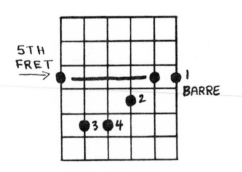

A aug

A dim

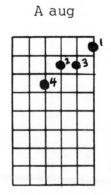

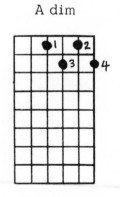

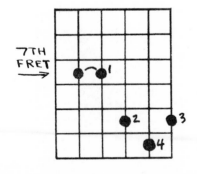

A

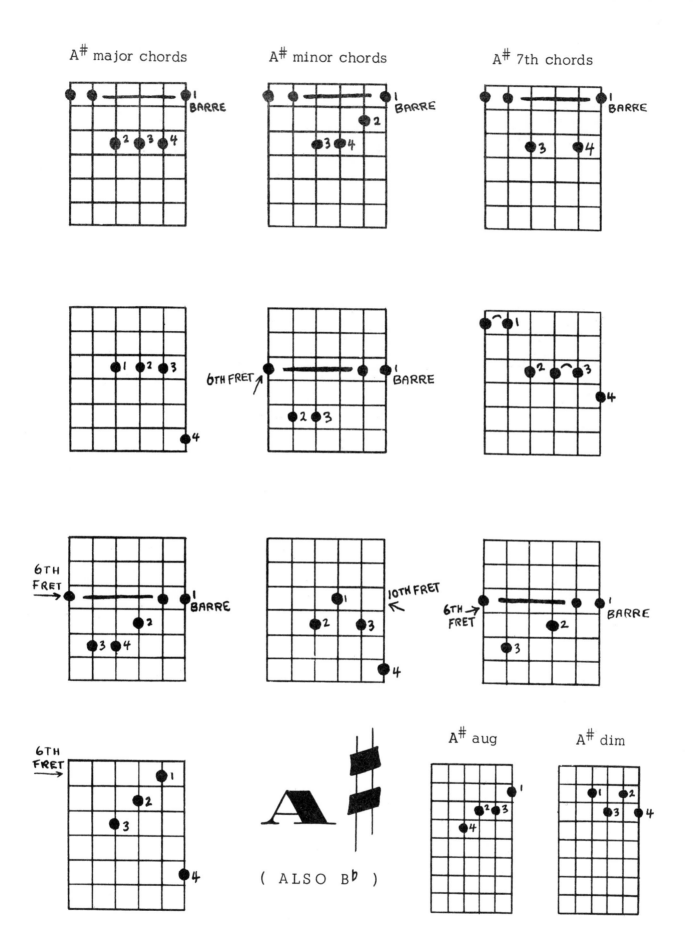

A# major chords

A# minor chords

A# 7th chords

6TH FRET

BARRE

BARRE

BARRE

6TH FRET

BARRE

10TH FRET

6TH FRET

BARRE

6TH FRET

(ALSO B♭)

A# aug

A# dim

B major   B minor chords   B 7th chords

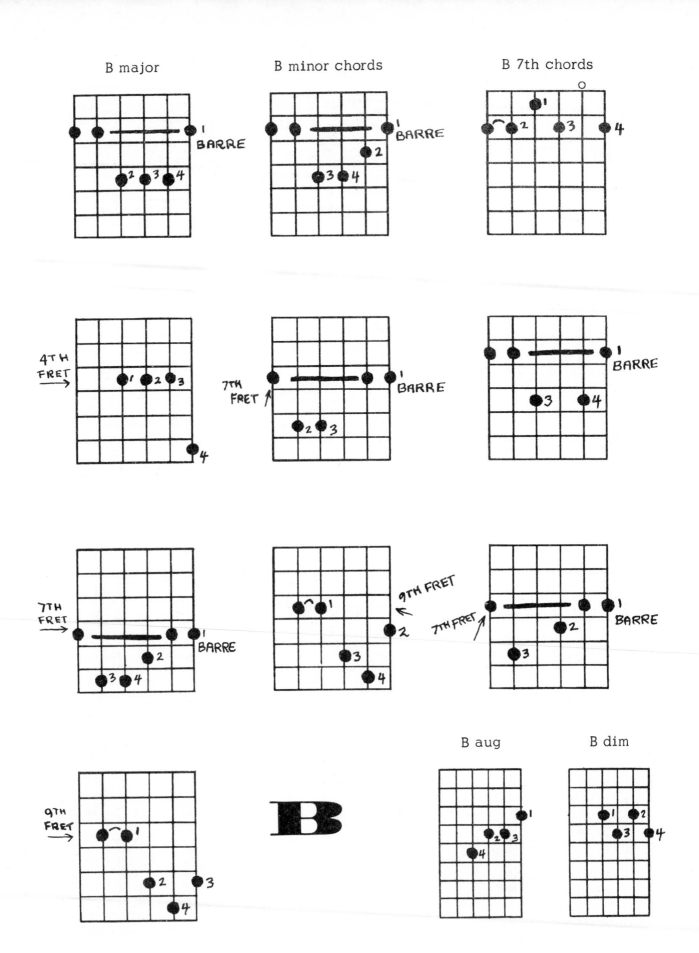

157

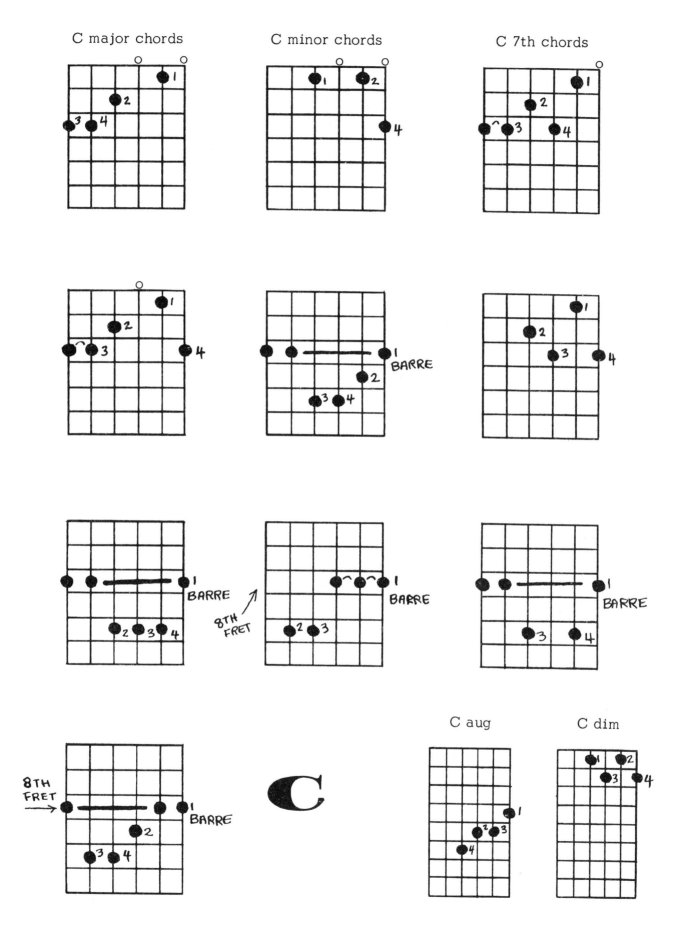

C major chords   C minor chords   C 7th chords

C aug   C dim

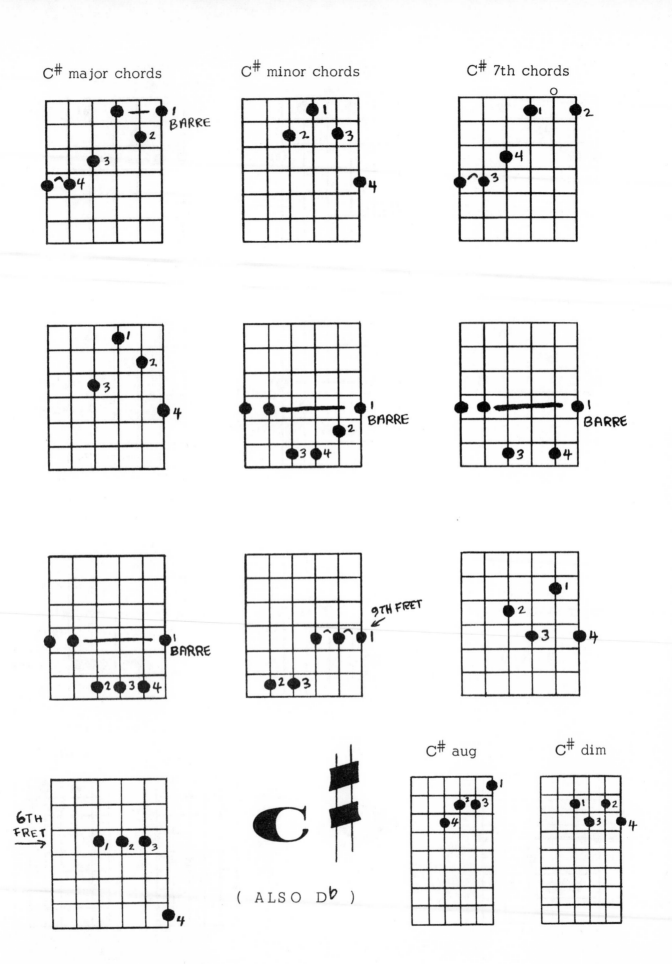

D major chords   D minor chords   D 7th chords

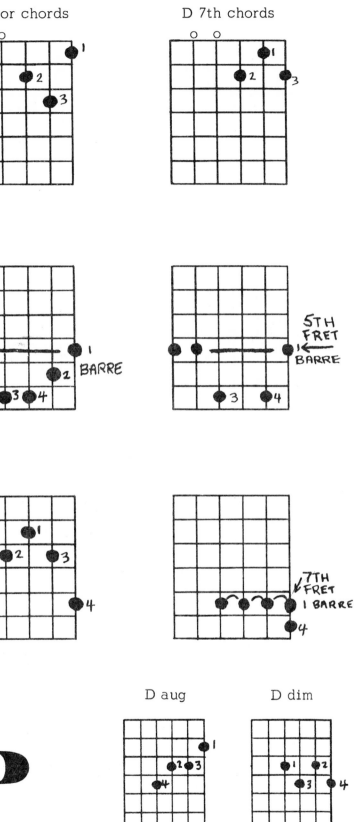

D

D aug   D dim

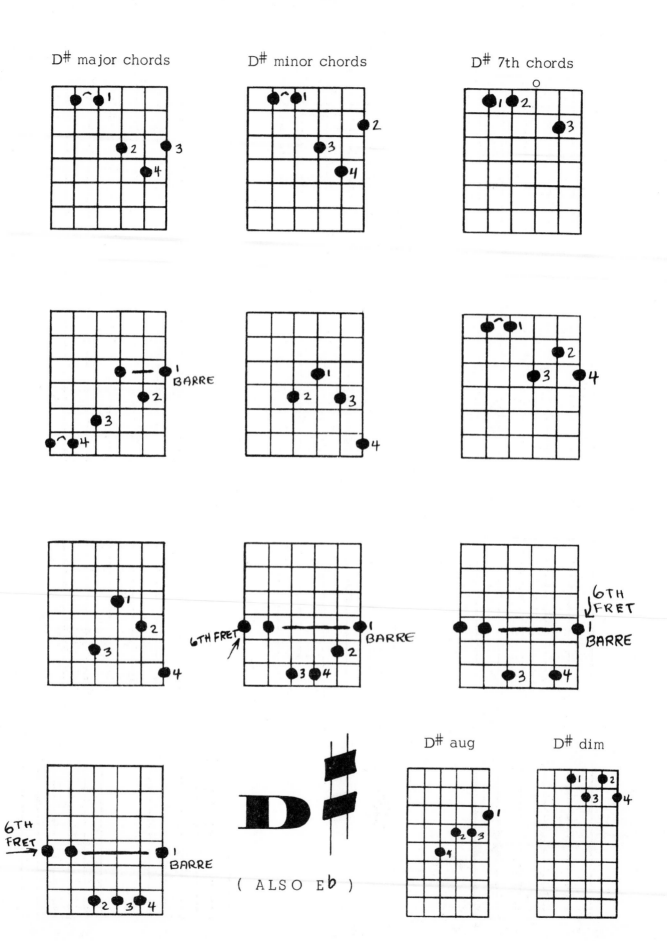

D# major chords

D# minor chords

D# 7th chords

6TH FRET
BARRE

6TH FRET
BARRE

6TH FRET
BARRE

6TH FRET
BARRE

D#

(ALSO E♭)

D# aug

D# dim

E major chords

E minor chords

E 7th chords

E aug

E dim

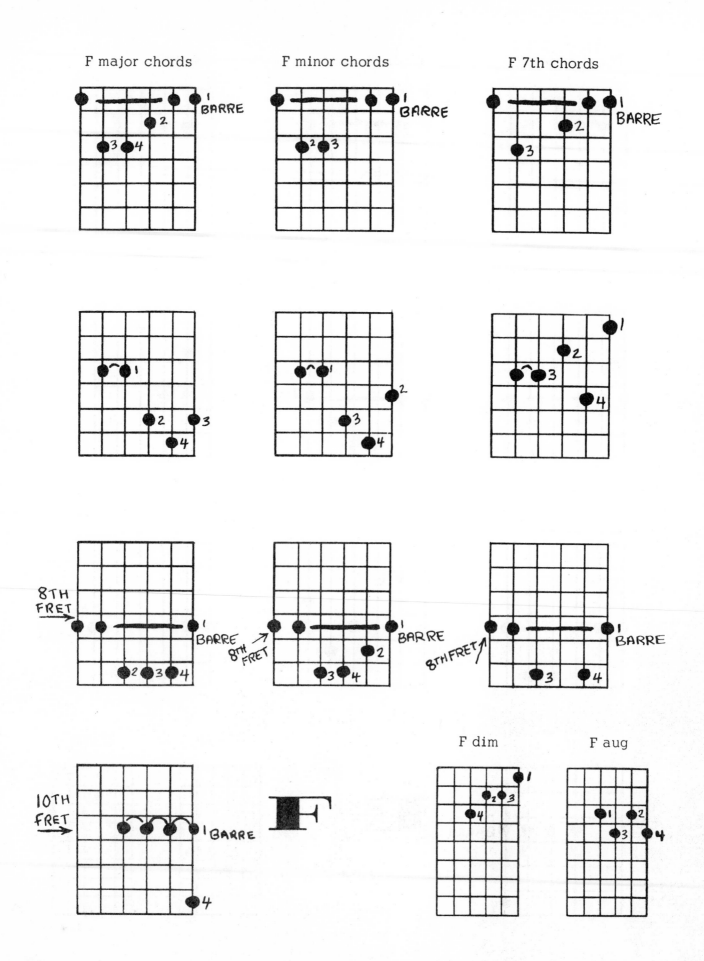

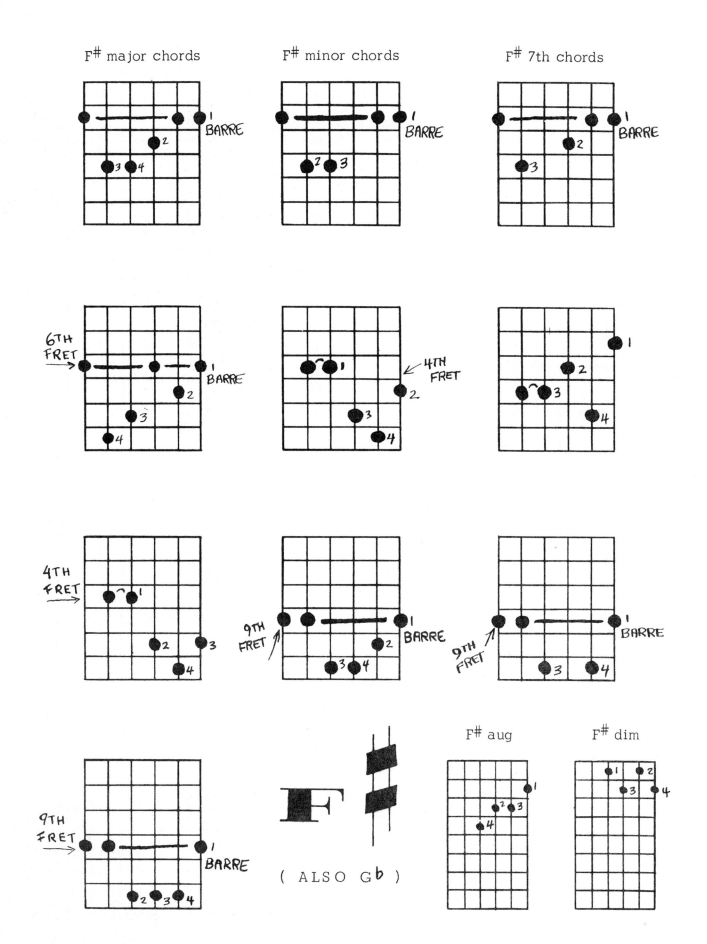

F# major chords

F# minor chords

F# 7th chords

6TH FRET → BARRE

← 4TH FRET

4TH FRET →

9TH FRET →

9TH FRET →

BARRE

9TH FRET →

BARRE

(ALSO G♭)

F# aug

F# dim

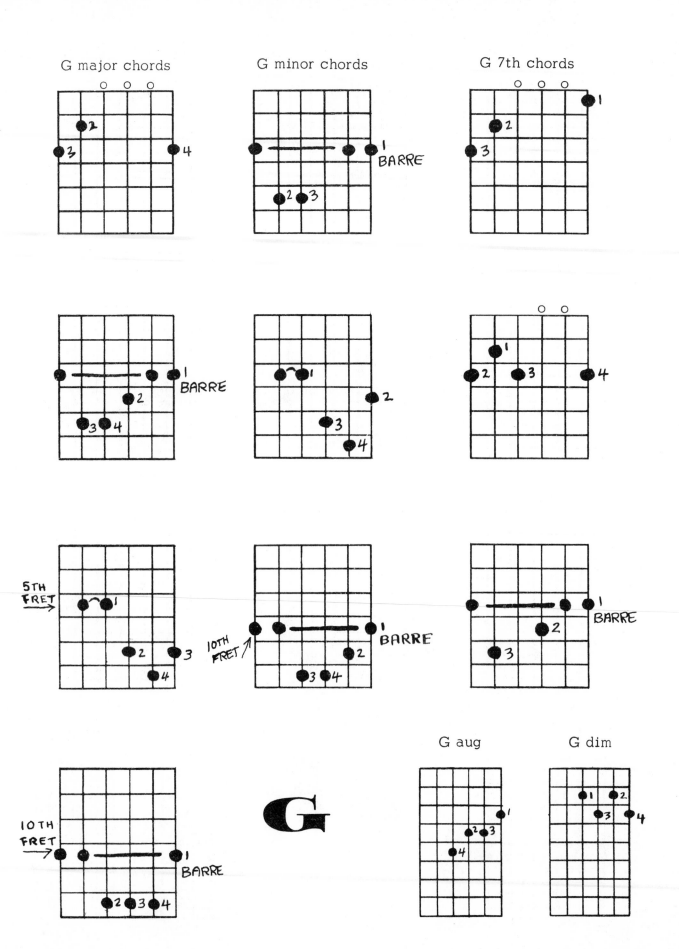

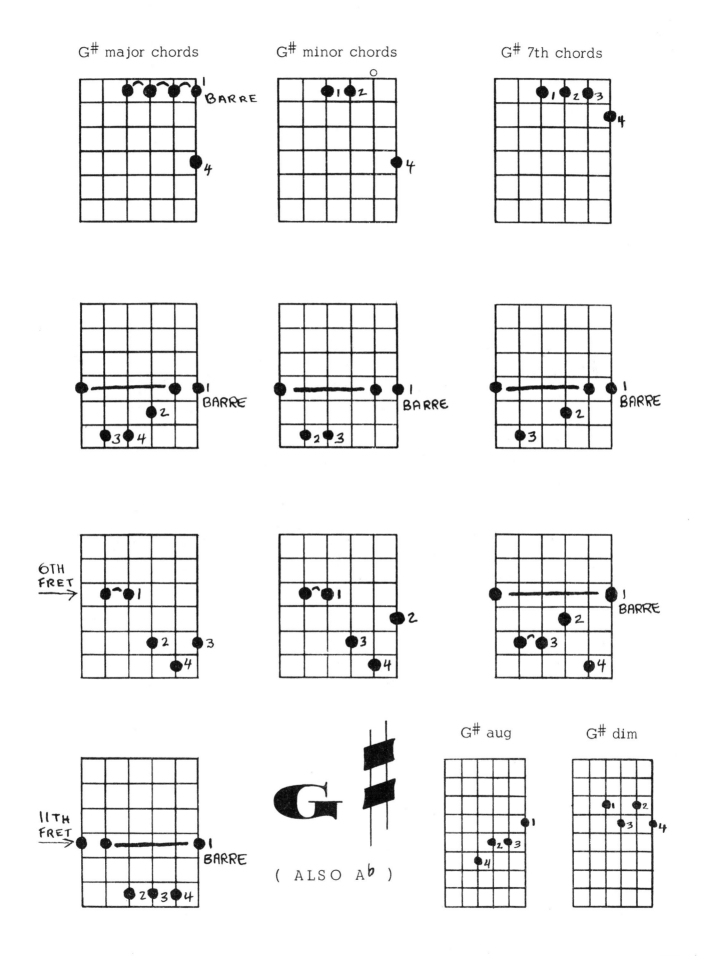